MANAGERIAL CHALLENGES IN BANKING

MANAGERIAL CHALLENGES IN BANKING

By

K.S. RAMACHANDRAN

ANMOL PUBLICATIONS PVT. LTD.

NEW DELHI - 110 002 (INDIA)

ANMOL PUBLICATIONS PVT. LTD.
4374/4B, Ansari Road, Daryaganj
New Delhi - 110 002
Ph.: 3261597, 3278000
www.anmolbooks.com

Managerial Challenges in Banking

First Edition, 2002

ISBN 81-261-1150-X

PRINTED IN INDIA

Published by J.L. Kumar for Anmol Publications Pvt. Ltd., New Delhi - 110 002 and Printed at Mehra Offset Press, Delhi.

CONTENTS

FOCUSSING THE ISSUES

Banking has been a core area of the development process since Independence. It has undertaken several tasks consistent with the changing roles assigned to it over the years. The 1969 nationalisation of 14 banks and the 1980 takeover of another six banks, followed by Mrs. Indira Gandhi's 20 point programme, rendered banks a major instrument of development activity.

Apart from being the financier of the Government – through investments in treasury bills and securities / bonds – the public sector constituents had to take up what came to be known as the priority sector lending. Support to Government and the designated priority sectors grew so much as to become a burden, with RBI's own reports regularly voicing concern over the reduced lendable resources. In Mrs. Gandhi's time, the loan melas gave banking activity a strong populist direction.

With reform, it became incumbent on the Government to provide a commercial orientation to banking practices and operations. Rightly, the first Narasimhan Committee in its report in November 1991 set the reform agenda for banks. Among other things, the committee mooted a phased reduction in the statutory liquidity ratio (SLR) – which was the means to bank financing of the Government sector's needs – and also a cut in priority sector lending. In September, 1994, an accord was reached between RBI and the Union Finance Ministry to phase out over a period RBI credit to the Central Government.

But, bank managers still have to meet the needs of priority sectors. As of now, 40 per cent of the gross bank credit of public sector banks goes to these sectors. The foreign and private sector banks also provide support to these sectors, though at a lower level.

The study seeks to examine the tasks of bank managers in a difficult global environment. Managers have to do much more than lending and borrowing. Derivatives have become a major challenge. I sincerely hope that I have helped focus on the tasks of managerial personnel in a situation where banking is increasingly acquiring a global character.

—K.S. Ramachandran

PREFACE

The present study is a logical extension of the publication, "*Managerial Challenges of Reform*", brought out earlier by me as part of my research endeavour. In fact, I had toyed with it even when I took up that project. Banking is an area that needed a strong dose of reform, if not sooner at least simultaneously with the various segments of the industrial sector. In its defence, it must be said that the political regime, which set the Indian economy a reform agenda, had not quite neglected the financial sector. Rather, it wasted no time in constituting the Narasimham Committee to lay down the priorities of this sector in a liberalising environment.

But, a decade after the economy was put on the reform path banking remains an area that is only peripherally touched by the reform policy. Less said about the spirit the better. While the infotech sector has benefited hugely from the Government's efforts to open up the economy, despite all the recommendations of the Narasimham Committee banking continues to be controlled by the Government and bureaucratically run. The time taken by the Union Cabinet to take a policy decision on reducing the Government's stake and, even more so, the reluctance even at the start of 2001 to undertake a course of privatisation — this was explicit in the strategy that it had opted for in November, 2000 — sent out a message that was none too encouraging.

The reasons are not merely obvious; these are, indeed, glaring. The unions, which still call the shots, do not want any change in the ***status quo***. While the world over, human resource management is identified with promoting a staff that is both leaner and meaner, the unions here have successfully resisted such an identification. This is not all. The Government is not also ready to accept a situation where banks cease to meet its needs on a mandatory basis. Banks have a substantial social obligation and there seems little likelihood of this being reduced in the near future.

Although the Narasimham Committee did call for a phased cut in the statutory liquidity ratio and in the level of priority sector lending, which largely constitute the banks' social burden, the Government has moved only haltingly towards this end. The ratio has been reduced, but is still high enough to pre-empt a good part of the scheduled commercial banks' demand and time liabilities. The banks do not get a good, even fair, return on what they lend to the Government sector, but true liberalisation should mean a freedom of choice on investments and banks should put a portion of the deposits they collect in Government and approved securities wholly by choice and not by pressure of mandate or under duress. At the very extreme of reform, perhaps the banks might even want to choose between refinancing by RBI and other, cheaper, options in regard to their lending resource base.

In this work, several issues have been addressed. I have taken recourse to the reports of the Union Finance Ministry, the Reserve Bank of India, the Bank of International Settlements, World Bank, IMF and the Punjab National Bank. But, the responsibility for the focussing of issues and the presentation is wholly mine. A seminar held jointly by IMF and World Bank in early 2000 had sought to grapple with the problems of sticky loans and the options open to banks in easing the related strains. For their part, the norms set by the Bank of International Settlements on banking supervision underscored the complexity of supervision.

My own two previous books on the 1991-92 securities

scandal – which itself had been discussed at the Faculty of Management Studies, Delhi University in early, 1992 – and on financial sector reform (Anmol, 1993) – discussed at the Indian Institute of Public Administration in 1993 – helped me to focus on the agenda set for banks. My research study on compulsions of fiscal management prepared for the Economic & Scientific Research Foundation in 1995 – the book was released at the National Council of Applied Economic Research by the then RBI Governor, Dr. C. Rangarajan and discussed by the then Chief Economic Advisor to the Union Finance Ministry, Dr. Shankar Acharya – provided the background to the fiscal connection to banking.

Obviously, neither academic discourses nor policy and administrative dictates are really going to help very much and managements and supervisors alike have to fight very hard to keep the different banking entities on a fairly even keel and also free of the kind of situations that often culminate in crises and scandals. We in India have had our share of such situations.

In my thrust on *Managerial Challenges in Banking*, I have been helped by several people at different levels, both within and outside the country. I have received substantial expert support from abroad, but those who made this possible will remain unnamed because of their professional commitments and the sensitive nature of their assignments. The current Chairman of the Indian Banks' Association and the Chairman of Punjab National Bank, Mr. S. S. Kohli has been a constant source of encouragement ever since I first met him on May 17, 2000. He has been kind enough to write the introduction to the study. Several senior officials of the Bank, Mr. A. Balasubramanian amd Mr. Gowda, both Deputy General Managers in the head office of the Bank, Dr. Lalitha Venkataramani and Mr B. Natarajan, both Assistant General Managers, have gone out of their way to brief me. I would like to thank them all. Mr. Radhakrishnan of the Bank's Management Advisory Services Division has also lent support to my efforts. Mr. C. N. Ardhanari, who has spent long years training bank managers and is presently involved in bank audit, has helped in my focussing the core issues. Mr. A. L. Seshadri with considerable experience as a bank manager has made my task easy by identifying the various hazards of staff at middle and senior levels. Mr. R. Y. Seshan, a banking software expert, has touched a key area of banking operations, that is his orbit. Mr. Krishna Murari Sinha has given exemplary secretarial assistance.

—K. S. Ramachandran

I

INTRODUCTION: MEASURING UP TO THE TASKS AHEAD

By S S Kohli,
Chairman, Indian Banks Association and
Chairman & Managing Director
Punjab National Bank
New Delhi

PRE-REFORM SCENARIO

From its early beginnings in the 18th century, modern banking in India has come a long way to grow into a mature and stable banking system. In the Indian financial system (IFS), the banking system (BS) occupies a predominant position. Till 1969 when the first set of 14 private banks were nationalised, banking business was mainly directed towards the more remunerative commercial and industrial segments of the economy, which came to be known as class banking. However, in the post-nationalisation era, there was a paradigm shift in economic ideology, and public sector banks were mandated to act as catalysts of economic development and poverty alleviation by promoting self-employment. Thus, began the era of mass banking eventually leading to extension of banking facilities throughout the length and breadth of the country.

In the new dispensation, banks were to balance their social role and commercial orientation and yet remain profitable. In 1980, six more banks were nationalised, taking the total of public sector banks to 28 including the State Bank of India and its seven subsidiaries. This led to a further concentration of banking business in the public sector, and by the nineties, the public sector banks accounted for over ninety per cent of banking business in India. During this period, a few private sector banks and foreign banks co-existed in the industry accounting for the rest of the banking business.

The growth process was predominantly directed by the State and the public sector banks came to sub-serve the larger interests of State policy. While the massive expansion of bank branches provided the much needed fillip to the banking habits of the population, extension of bank credit formed an important element of the programme of poverty eradiction. Directed credit programmes with preferential interest rates led to a substantial cross-subsidisation, while the Government used bank resources for funding its large public expenditure. The large pre-emption of bank resources, which at one point exceeded 63 per cent, led to an automatic monetisation of fiscal deficit. Total regulation of interest rates, which were more often pegged at artificially low levels, prescription of credit ceilings and directed credit programmes led to a financial repression and distortions in allocation of resources. As a result, banks worked under a protective environment and the quality of service steadily deteriorated. In the absence of transparency in their operations,banks booked incomes, which were not realised; while the cost factors were given a go by, profitability was relegated to the background and banks were saddled with assets of poor quality. Eventually, the costs became unsustainable and some of the banks started incurring losses and accumulated these to the extent of wiping away their entire networth.

THE REFORM AGENDA

In 1990-91, the Indian economy faced an unprecedented external crisis arising out of macro-economic imbalances. The unsustainable fiscal deficit and the ill-effects of the Gulf war took its toll on the economy, already plagued by an overvalued exchange rate, high tariffs, inefficiencies in industrial sector and a financially repressed banking sector. A resolution of the imbalances was attempted through the twin process of stabilisation in the short term and structural reform over the medium and long term. The structural changes *inter alia* related to sweeping changes in industry, foreign trade, taxation, etc. Reforms in the financial sector, which also progressed simultaneously, formed an important part of the overall structural adjustment of the Indian economy. To restore external competitiveness and to correct the overvaluation of the rupee, the exchange rate was adjusted downwards in two stages in 1991 by a cumulative 18 per cent.

Although attempts had been made earlier to bring about changes in the financial sector, a cohesive strategy for reforms came only with the report of the Narasimham Committee (1991). The broad aim of the reform process was clear. With the gradual opening up of the economy, the financial sector cannot be kept in isolation. Accordingly, a movement from financial repression to liberalisation had to be achieved through a shift from an interventionist approach to market-based mechanisms. This was to facilitate an improvement in operational efficiency i.e., reduction in costs of financial intermediation and allocational efficiency i.e., allocation of resources to the best possible uses. This paradigm shift towards deregulation and liberalisation have brought about several managerial challenges. Banks are increasingly facing competition and as technology makes deeper inroads, the contours of financial sector are getting redefined. However, the managerial challenges in the banking sector can be best understood by first discussing some aspects of the reforms.

The reforms in the banking sector have been implemented under three broad categories:

- Policy environment within which banks operate,

interest rates, pre-emption of resources, directed lending etc.

- Initiatives to improve the financial health of banks through prescription of prudential norms, capital adequacy, removal of structural barriers to entry and fostering competition between banks.
- Institutional strengthening by establishment of suitable regulatory and supervisory mechanisms and modifying the legal framework.

To quote Dr C Rangarajan, former Governor, Reserve Bank of India, " the central objective of reform in the financial sector has been to improve the efficiency, competitiveness and productivity of the system".

The first phase of reforms proved to be successful and it was non-disruptive. This had given confidence for launching the second generation reforms, which was mapped out by the same committee (Narasimham Committee 1998).

PRUDENTIAL REGULATION

Before the reform process, the banks were booking incomes on an accrual basis and to the extent banks were booking incomes which were unrealised, their balance sheets did not reflect their true position. In other words, the capital and reserves position of banks were overvalued since provisioning for loan losses was almost non-existent. This could not be sustained because ultimately the loan losses have to be written off against capital and reserves, which in turn would jeopardise the interests of depositors of the banks. Therefore, the initial reform measures centred on cleansing the balance sheets of banks.

This was achieved by implementation of internationally accepted prudential accounting norms, according to which assets have to be classified into four categories viz., standard, sub-standard, doubtful and loss. Further, income recognition from loan assets should be on a realised rather than an accrual basis. Other than standard assets, the rest are treated as non-performing (NPA) and no interest should be charged to or taken into account from these assets. The classification will have to be done on the basis of degree of credit-weaknesses and the dependence on collateral for purposes of realisation of dues. Depending upon the classification, provisioning will have to be made ranging between 10 per cent (in case of sub-standard assets) and 100 per cent in case of loss assets. While initially the prudential norms were liberal, gradually the rigours of asset classification have been made more stringent. Currently, if interest in a loan account remains unpaid for two quarters from the date it has become due, it will be treated as NPA. Further, from fiscal year 1999-2000, banks will have to make a general provision of 0.25 per cent in respect of standard assets. The trend in the asset quality of public sector banks after implementation of the prudential accounting norms is given below.

Loan Asset Quality of Public sector bank group

(per cent)

Category	*1994*	*1995*	*1996*	*1997*	*1998*	*1999*	*2000*
1. Standard Assets	75.2	80.6	82	82.2	84	84.1	86
2. Sub- Standard Assets	7.4	3.9	4	5.1	5.1	4.9	4.3
3. Doubtful Assets	14.1	11.6	10.7	10.6	9.1	9	8
4. Loss Assets	2.4	1.9	1.9	2.1	1.9	2	1.7
5. NPA in advances with o/s of < Rs 25000	0.9	2	1.4	*	*	*	*
6. Total NPAs (2 to 5)	24.8	19.4	18	17.8	16	15.9	14
7. Total Advances (1+6)	100	100	100	100	100	100	100

* Since included in overall position

Source: Report on Trend & Progress of Banking, RBI, 1999-2000

Gross NPAs of public sector banks at the end of March 2000 were Rs. 53,500 crore or 14.3 per cent of gross advances.

However, the level of NPAs in the Indian banking industry should be seen in the light of a larger overhang arising out of historical reasons and non-availability of means for quick recovery of dues from non-performing loans. Fourteen debt recovery tribunals (DRTs) and three (Appellate) DRATs have been established to facilitate quick enforcement of bank securities. Besides, one more DRT and 2 DRATs are being established. At the end of December, 1999, there were 35,600 cases with DRTs involving about Rs. 45,000 crore. Sufficient administrative and financial powers have been delegated to the presiding officers to enable them to function more effectively. However, the effectiveness of the DRTs has been far from satisfactory. Another important step for resolving the NPAs has been the implementation of settlement advisory committees (SAC) and effective till March 2001. Under this RBI scheme, banks could arrive at a negotiated settlement with defaulting borrowers of upto Rs. 5 crore. This is a form of debt forgiveness and banks have been able to make significant progress in reducing their NPAs through this route.

CAPITAL ADEQUACY

The ownership of public sector banks by the Government has acted as a pillar of confidence, even though some banks reported losses after the implementation of prudential norms. However, as losses have to be eventually set against capital and reserves, prudence demands that banks have adequate cushion to meet such contingencies. Moreover, in a deregulated environment, there is a vital need to link risk-exposure with capital funds. Following the Narasimham Committee recommendations, a system of capital adequacy was implemented modeled on the lines suggested by the Basel Committee on capital convergence. Accordingly, all banks were required to attain a minimum CRAR of nine per cent by March 2000. Moreover, banks are on notice to implement some of the recommendations of the Narasimham Committee (1998) with regard to assigning risk weight on (a) Government securities; (b) market risks; (c) and open positions in forex and gold.

Frequency Distribution of Capital Adequacy norms by banks

Bank Group	*Below 4 per* cent	*Between 4 - 8 per* cent	*Between 8 - 10 per* cent	*Above 10 per* cent
1. State Bank of India (SBI)	-	-	-	1
2. SBI Associates	-	-	-	7
3. Nationalised Banks	1	-	4	14
Total	**1**	**-**	**4**	**22**

Source: Report on Trend & Progress of banking, RBI, 1999-2000

In the wake of implementation of prudential accounting norms and capital adequacy, a large gap arose which the nationalised banks had to meet. As owner, the Government undertook a programme of recapitalisation involving over Rs. 204.46 billion upto March 31, 1999.During 1999-2000, no recapitalisation was provided, although one of the banks was allowed to write down part of its capital to adjust for losses.

The financially sound banks have continued to remain profitable, even after implementing the stipulated prudential norms. Since the resource gap for strengthening the capital base of banks is large, the Government desired that the financially sound banks approach the capital market for raising funds. This called for modifications in current banking law.

An amendment to the State Bank of India Act, 1955 and the introduction of the Banking Companies (Acquisition and Transfer of Undertaking) Amendment Bill, 1994 were effected. As per these changes, the paid-up capital of banks can be raised through public issue of shares subject to the condition, that at all times the Central Government would continue to hold not less than 51 per cent of the paid-up capital. Some of the banks have already raised long term resources from the market to augment their capital base. In fact, in the case of most such banks, part of the Government capital has been returned and no contributions to the capital base from the Government is envisaged. The ultimate objective is to disinvest government holding upto the prescribed level. Towards this end, the Government has already announced that it would reduce its share holding to 33 per cent while keeping the public sector character unchanged.

STRUCTURAL REGULATION

Structural regulation broadly refers to norms relating to entry of new banks, licensing of branches etc. With the system of prudential regulation in place, structural regulation in the banking sector has been relaxed. The norms for entry of private sector banks were announced way back in January 1993. The minimum paid-up capital of these banks should be Rs.1 billion right at the beginning and step were to be covered by the prudential regulation norms as mentioned above. These banks were to have no restrictions on using state-of-the-art technology and opening branches.

Nine such private banks were established (with a merger between HDFC Bank and Times Bank, the number now stands at eight) including those by some of the public sector financial institutions. Although this has not led to competition immediately, the market is getting segmented. With the use of sophisticated work technology, these banks are concentrating presently in the metropolitan areas targeting corporate and high-value clients, besides engaging in forex and related operations. Further diversification into areas like custodial services, stock-broking etc. are also likely and with their progressive growth, competitive forces are expected to become pronounced in the coming years. In the recent period, the process of consolidation amongst these newly established private banks have begun. The consolidation efforts are expected to strengthen in the near future.

REDUCTION IN STATUTORY PRE-EMPTIONS

In terms of Section 42 (1) of the Reserve Bank of India Act, banks are required to hold an amount not less than three per cent of their total demand and time liabilities (DTL) as average daily balance in the form of cash balances with RBI, which otherwise is termed as cash reserve ratio **(CRR)**. Similarly, as per Section 24 of the Banking Regulation Act, banks are required to maintain a certain portion of their DTL, which will be invested in Government paper and other approved securities under the statutory liquidity ratio **(SLR)**. These reserve requirements are part of the instruments of monetary control by the RBI. With the Government's fiscal deficit remaining at high levels over the years, these pre-emptions were used to fund Government's public expenditure. At the same time, the rate of return for the banks was low. These pre-emptions were progressively increased over a period of time and by 1991, these two ratios put together reached as high as 63.5 per cent. Such high levels of pre-emptions of banks' resources had the deleterious effect of automatic monetisation of fiscal deficit, high inflation, crowding-out private sector demand for credit and seriously eroding the profit position of public sector banks.

As part of the reform process, the RBI targeted to reduce SLR and is moving towards this end in phases. At present, the SLR stands reduced to 25 per cent of DTL, which is the minimum level as per the Banking Regulation Act. Similarly CRR at present has been reduced to eight per cent. The objective of reduction in these reserve requirements is to release additional resources for the banks, which could be profitably deployed in lending. At the same time, Government has moved towards raising its resources at market-related interest rates, with the result the yield on Government paper has shown an improvement. To facilitate the development of a Government paper market and money market, RBI has introduced various structural measures with the objective of achieving full integration of the financial markets.

DE-REGULATION OF INTEREST RATES

Rationalisation of the interest rate structure has been carried out gradually with the ultimate objective of total deregulation of interest rates. The most important reform in the interest rate structure was the deregulation of lending rates on advances above Rs 0. 2 million. With a predominant portion of loans falling in this category, banks have been given freedom to fix the interest rates, depending upon the risk perception of the loan. For this, banks have to evolve a prime lending rate (PLR), which will be the rate offered to the first-class clients of the banks and peg the interest rates to be charged for other borrowers to this base rate. Banks have been required to declare the maximum spread they earn over the PLR. Loans in the Rs. 25,000 - 0.2 million category will be charged at PLR.

In order to switch to indirect signal-based tools of monetary control, the RBI has activated the bank rate, which is the rate at which the central bank discounts eligible bills. Interest rates are getting gradually linked to the bank rate and this rate has been reduced to seven per cent on March 1, 2001. Keeping with such a falling interest rate regime, many banks have reduced their PLR to the lowest level achieved so far. To curb emergence of an usurious rate of interest, banks are required to declare the maximum spread they earn over the PLR. Loans upto Rs. 0.2 million will be charged not beyond PLR. From October, 1994, lending rates were deregulated for all loans and advances excepting those under the differential rate of interest (DRI) scheme, export credit and advances upto Rs.0.2 million. Banks were also permitted to announce their prime term lending rate (PTLR) for term loans over Rs.0. 2 million. In respect of deposit rates also, interest rates have been more or less deregulated with banks being allowed to determine interest rates on all term deposits. Interest rates on saving deposits are still regulated, but this is also expected to be deregulated eventually. Thus, the process of deregulation of interest rates has been more or less achieved, save for certain categories of loans and saving deposits. The deregulation process during the last decade has provided valuable lessons to banks, particularly in regard to cost consciousness in resource mobilisation.

DIRECTED CREDIT AND RURAL FINANCE

Considering the contribution of agriculture and the rural sector to the national economy, a multi-agency approach to rural credit and development has been adopted. The rural credit system in the Indian context has been a product of both evolution and active intervention by the Government. Bank credit to the rural sector is denominated under priority sector credit, under which various target groups of beneficiaries are included. These *inter alia* include credit to agriculture and allied activities, small scale industries and credit to weaker sections, professionals and the self-employed. Various poverty alleviation programmes aimed at the rural sector are also included in this programme.

At the end of March 2000, public sector banks exceeded the targeted lending for priority sectors to reach 43.6 per cent and amounted to Rs. 1278 billion. While of the total branches of commercial banks, nearly 52 per cent were in rural areas, out of the total deposits held by them, 15 per cent came from rural areas; in terms of credit deployment, the banking system deployed more than 11 per cent of its credit in the rural segment. To augment the efforts of public sector banks in lending to rural areas, the inflow of resources to the National Bank for Agriculture and Rural Development (NABARD) has been increased considerably.

Significant changes have been brought about in the definition of priority sector by broadening the coverage and combining the sub-goals relating to direct/indirect agriculture credit. The concessionality element in interest rates on these loans have also been largely done away with, thereby reducing the burden of cross-subsidisation for banks. To provide a level playing field, foreign banks are also required to dispense priority sector credit, so are the new private sector banks.

Balancing social orientation with achievement of adequate profits, obviously, is a challenge before the banks.

FINANCIAL SUPERVISION

With deregulation, the supervisory role of the Reserve Bank of India has been enhanced. Following the recommendations of the Narasimham Committee, a separate Board for Supervision (BFS) has been established. Besides, a Department of Supervision (DoS) headed by a Deputy Governor has been established. The DoS has been entrusted with the task of supervising the banks and other non-banking financial companies. A process of rating banks on the **CAMELS (Capital adequacy, Management, Earnings, Liquidity and Systems)** format has been put in place.

Keeping with the shift towards prudential regulation, emphasis is being laid on off-site supervision, which will supplement the on-site supervision. The off-site supervision system comprises 12 returns focussing on the supervisory concerns like capital adequacy, asset quality, credit concentration, connected lending, risk exposure etc. The role of reporting accountants has been enhanced so as to improve the authenticity of the data reported, while measures have also been initiated to strengthen internal governance in banks. Particular mention may be made of the system of concurrent audit of large branches of banks and the constitution of the audit committee of the board (ACB). Banks already have the system of executive committee (EC) and management committee (MC) to make important operational decisions.

RISK MANAGEMENT

With progressive deregulation of interest rates, risk management has assumed paramount importance. The Reserve Bank of India has issued guidelines to banks to introduce a system of asset-liability management (ALM) to address market risks like interest rate risks, exchange rate risk etc. Although this is in its infancy, the ALM system is expected to stabilise quickly and the introduction of risk hedging instruments like interest rate swaps are facilitating the process. The comprehensive risk management guidelines of RBI also cover credit risk management, under which banks have been required to take various initiatives to address default risk and portfolio risk. Development of credit rating tools, credit scoring models, preventive monitoring systems, loan audit etc have also been suggested by the RBI. Besides, banks are required to address operational risks arising out of the failure of computer systems, weaknesses in internal control etc. Accordingly, as part of internal governance, banks have constituted the Asset Liability Management Committee (ALCO) and Credit Risk Management Committee (CRMC).

Towards improving transparency and to achieve better disclosure of the banks' balance sheet, the information provided therein has been enhanced. Accordingly, banks are required to disclose the break-up of provisions made towards NPAs, depreciation on investments and capital adequacy. From March 2000, banks are required to disclose:

- the maturity pattern of loans and advances, investments, deposits and borrowings;
- the foreign currency assets and liabilities
- the movement in NPAs and provisions
- the lending to sensitive sectors

With liberalisation, the focus has shifted to prudential regulation aimed at promoting safety and soundness of the banking system. Towards this end, the RBI has accepted the Core Principles for Effective Supervision (1997) evolved by the BIS and eventually the accounting standards as envisaged by the International Accounting Standards Committee (IASC) for loan valuation and credit loss provisioning could also be accepted. RBI constituted various working groups for the purpose on payment systems, preventive corrective action, financial regulation and supervision, transparency in monetary policy, accounting standards etc. RBI advised banks to annex the balance sheet of their subsidiaries beginning March 2001 so that a gradual move towards consolidation of balance sheets could be made.

EMERGING TRENDS

The twin forces driving the international banking business currently are consolidation and convergence. As a result, many banking systems are moving towards an universal banking model to realise scope economies and scale. This trend has created some of the world's biggest banks with a huge balance sheet. Thus, the current paradigm is: Size Matters. As the phenomenon of bank gigantism expands, at the other extreme, technology is emerging as a key driver. The advances in computers and telecom have revolutionised the financial sector and banking on the net is fast catching on. As e-commerce gets transformed into m-commerce with the increasing use of technologies like WAP (Wireless Application Protocol), banking business is in for a major overhaul. Customers, realising the benefits of technology, are demanding more for less. They expect speedier and prompt financial services and technology-enabled banking solutions. As physical network is replaced by virtual alternatives, the existence of brick-and-mortar branches are called into question. The mega banks believe that their brand strength will help them survive such technological advancements. This has led to a sharper focus on brand management by many of the multinational banks.

TOWARDS UNIVERSAL BANKING

The first phase of India's financial reforms highlighted may be termed curative inasmuch as these were addressed to the issue of cleansing the balance sheets of banks and putting these on a recovery path. The second generation reforms will be preventive, aimed at building a strong and robust banking system, which can withstand the pressures of globalisation. The broad tenor of the recommendations of the second Narasimham Committee is to move towards universal banking. This view has been echoed by the RBI also. The opening of the Indian insurance sector will usher in bancassurance. The development finance institutions (DFIs) like IDBI, ICICI have espoused their cause for converting themselves into universal banks. They have moved in this direction by setting up commercial bank ventures. In a way, it also indicates that the Indian banking system is not immune from the trends holding sway in the global financial scenario.

It has been suggested that the twin forces of consolidation and convergence need to be reckoned within the Indian context. Possibilities of convergence have been envisaged through universal banking to lead to one-stop financial supermarkets providing a range of services such as commercial, merchant and investment banking and even insurance. Risk diversification is also expected to be achieved through convergence, resulting in strengthening of the system. In essence, the suggestions are aimed at establishing financial conglomerates through a process of mergers and diversification. The first and foremost condition for attainment of capital account convertibility will be strengthening the banking system, which in turn would call for a higher size of balance sheet so that Indian banks can withstand the pressures of international competition. But, it is felt that attainment of a bigger size should not be seen as a major driver of consolidation, especially from the point of view of systemic soundness.

At the same time, the supervisory structure will have to allow for financial diversification and innovation while attempting to contain risks within individual financial affiliates and preferably prevent any spillage of financial difficulties originating in a non-bank affiliate overflowing into the parent bank. It may be mentioned that the Reserve Bank of India, following the BIS model, has started moving towards the Three-Pillar Approach to regulation by strengthening internal governance, official oversight and market discipline. Whatever structure or model is adopted, ensuring safety and soundness of the banking system will be the main challenge. Stricter prudential regulation, better disclosures, market discipline, improved internal governance and effective official oversight will provide the approach for meeting such a challenge.

ON A LEARNING CURVE

With interest rates, more or less, deregulated and with competition gaining apace in different market segments, risk management is becoming crucial. So far, the public sector banks have been the beneficiaries of State protection and rule-based regulation and direction from the monetary authority. With a lack of clarity on their commercial role, banks have tended to ignore profitability. With the reforms and the gradual freedom that they have now been bestowed with, adjustment to the market-led conditions will have to be completed. Indian banks are, therefore, on a learning curve. The logical outcome of the strategy of deregulation and competition will be financial innovation and introduction of risk hedging mechanisms. Trends in disintermediation are already evident with the corporate sector accessing the capital market and issuing instruments like CPs. Once the economy shows a strong sign of revival, capital market activity is likely to pick up and disintermediation is likely to gain momentum. The process of financial innovations has also commenced recently with the introduction of interest rate swaps. But, this needs to be followed up by other derivative instruments. However, development of the full-fledged OTC market will take a longer time. A near absence of technology and skills have impaired the development of such markets and these impediments cannot be just wished away. There is a need to systematically address the structural issues so that the financial markets can attain full integration. With a suitable supervisory structure including proper legal systems and investor protection measures, the Indian financial market can graduate from an emerging market to an efficient market.

THE OPERATIONAL CHALLENGES

In a nutshell, the banking sector has to address the following issues:

- A high level of concentration of banking business within the public sector bank group has blunted competitive forces
- Clearing the huge overhang of NPAs within the public sector bank group is a major problem.
- Market discipline is almost absent
- Introduction of proper debt recovery mechanisms including insolvency procedures, bankruptcy laws and corporate debt restructuring (CDR) mechanism should be a priority.
- Resolution of distressed banks in the public sector
- Dilution of Government ownership in public sector banks
- Exit policy for enterprises
- Establishment of a real time gross settlement (RTGS) payment system
- Achievement of a full market integration
- Reduction in directed lending
- Better internal governance
- Resolving a multiplicity of regulatory agencies (RBI, SEBI, BFS, IRA)
- Financial innovations are absent; risk hedging mechanisms are inadequate
- Skills to work under market-led conditions are relatively underdeveloped.
- Low technology absorption

- Huge manpower and lower productivity

While the above issues merit individual discussion in view of their complexity and the managerial tasks they pose, at the bank level, the priorities can be narrowed down to the following:

- Rationalisation of manpower
- Use of technology
- Financial innovations

The huge manpower with the public sector banks needs to be rationalised if productivity is to increase. This is crucial since as much as 65 to 70 per cent of the total operating costs account for establishment expenses. As banks had either gone into an expansion spree following governmental dictates of catalsying economic growth and financing self-employment/ poverty alleviation schemes, recruitment of fresh hands was resorted to in a big way. However, since the initiation of financial reforms, recruitments have considerably slowed down. The average age profile of bank employees is a cause for concern. According to data available, 47 per cent is in the 36-46 years group while only 15 per cent is in the 25-35 years age group. Banks do not have the requisite autonomy to offer a compensation package to fresh talented recruits and, thus, face a non-level playing field *vis-a-vis* private and foreign banks.

OPTING FOR VRS

As part of rationalisation, the Narasimham Committee suggested a scheme for voluntary separation. Following the Government's encouragement, public sector banks have recently announced an attractive voluntary retirement scheme (VRS). This has been a major step as this was one of the most contentious issues facing the banking sector. The response to the VRS of most of the banks has been overwhelming, which reveals that if an attractive monetary package is provided and safeguards are taken not to lose good workers, the VRS can help in cutting down surplus manpower. With this, the golden handshake has been accepted as a downsizing (better still, rightsizing) tool in the public sector. The real managerial challenge lies in the aftermath of the VRS. Firstly, rationalisation of manpower will have to be achieved at the earliest so that the vacuum arising out of the exit of employees is filled up. This could also require relocation of staff in large numbers. Secondly, this could lead to de-layering aimed at cutting down organisation tiers and closure of unviable branches. Third, banks will have bear the financial impact of the severance package, which according to actuarial estimates will be in the range of Rs. 7000-Rs. 10,000 crore. The funding options in this respect need to be evolved. While the reduction in establishment costs arising out of VRS can be felt only in the medium term, this could also lead to a reduction in intermediation costs to some extent, the beneficiary of which will be the borrowers. With interest rates moving southwards, banks will have to learn to work with leaner staff and thinner margins. Banks should also ensure that due to shortage of manpower, the quality of customer service does not suffer. It appears that VRS could at best provide a partial solution to the issue of reduction in intermediation costs, as banks which are burdened with a huge backlog of NPAs will not be in a position to cut interest rates to the desired extent.

But, by far the most challenging task before banks in the post-VRS situation will be changing the mindset of employees to face up to the competitive pressures. This will call for a thorough reorientation of HR initiatives in the banks. The HR strategy, *inter alia*, will have to deal with career path, provision of incentives for better performance, training in areas like risk management, technology, marketing, relationship management etc. In other words, employees should be able to adopt a commercial orientation to business so that they can service existing clients well and recruit new customers. The reduction in manpower could also give a push to the use of technology.

Public sector banks have been late entrants in respect of technology, with the result that their level of technology absorption has been low. Recognising the need for using IT, the banks have gone for large scale computerisation of branches. More than 65,300 PCs and nodes in about 3,800 fully computerised branches have been installed. Besides, another 14,000 PCs have been installed in the controlling offices and HOs of banks along with 2745 LAN (Local Area Network) systems. Public sector banks have also been required to cover 70 per cent of their business through computerisation in terms of the guidelines of the Central Vigilance Commission.

TOWARDS HIGH LEVELS OF AUTOMATION

In contrast, the newer private sector banks have achieved high levels of automation and have started offering electronic banking products including mobile banking to their top-end customers. Although at a limited level some of the public sector banks have also moved towards electronic banking, which include stand-alone ATMs, shared ATM Networks, issue and distribution of plastic cards, telebanking, maintaining websites, on-line submission of loan applications etc., considering the vast customer base they serve, such strategies are clearly inadequate. Further, a lack of standardisation and non-availability of a reliable and safe inter-bank and intra-bank communication backbone have hampered any significant development of technology. With the recent establishment of INFINET (Indian Financial Network) by RBI, using V-SAT technology has begun. The INFINET will provide inter-bank connectivity and would eventually help in introduction of various electronic banking products addressed to different market segments. It is also envisaged that the implementation of the real time gross settlement (RTGS) system will be completed soon, bringing the payment systems in the country on par with other developed countries. However, growth of electronic banking is strongly predicated to the introduction of relevant legislation including EFT Act and Cyber laws. It may be mentioned that the Information Technology Bill,'99 *inter alia* provides for legal recognition of electronic records, digital signatures and books of account maintained in electronic form by a bank.

Therefore, public sector banks will have to focus on evolving alternative channels of service delivery like ATMs, electronic fund transfer (EFT), internet banking etc. Opening of new channels of delivery will call into question the desirability of maintaining a large branch network because adding another channel of delivery without pruning the existing channels like branch will only add to overheads. Since electronic service channels will drastically cut the costs of transactions, banks will be required to optimise their branch network and cut transaction costs.

TAKING UP INNOVATIONS

Closely linked to the use of technology are innovations. In fact, in the developed economies, technology has been a key driver of financial innovations. It was the advancement in computing and communications technology that spurred the growth of derivative instruments and cross-border transactions. In fact, technology is credited with ending geography, as funds today flow in a seamless world. Unbundling of risks has become possible with the use of technology-based solutions, a task which derivatives perform. As the process of deregulation is pursued and structural barriers are lowered, new opportunities will emerge. But, in every opportunity, there is an inherent risk as well. Banks cannot perform in a competitive environment unless there are means of mitigating the inherent risks. Derivative instruments like swaps, options, futures etc. enable such risk mitigation. As the Indian financial market moves towards greater sophistication, some of these instruments have emerged as in the case of interest rate swaps, futures etc. Securitisation is in its infancy. But, there is need for more such instruments considering the globalisation of the corporate sector and as the Indian economy overall integrates with the world economy. Acquiring the skills to offer such products will pose a major challenge to public sector banks. But, as mentioned earlier, development of full-fledged OTC markets will take some time as the structural rigidities in the financial markets are addressed.

At the retail level, public sector banks will have to make further inroads into electronic banking. It could be through card-based mechanisms like stored-value products (Smart Cards), internet based banking, telebanking, remote banking etc. This will lead to innovative technology-based products and services. As the Indian banks move gradually towards universal banking and as they position themselves as financial service providers, banking business is getting redefined. Technology is unsettling the earlier business processes and customer behaviour is undergoing a significant change. To survive under these conditions, the public sector banks will have to undertake business process re-engineering, redefine their strategy and align their organisation structure. They have to understand their core competencies and dovetail their strategies to exploit such strengths. Besides, banks will have to develop an IT strategy and also HR strategies, which are aligned to the overall business strategy. Banks which are successful in restructuring their operations will be better placed to face the onslaught of competition.

II

FROM A MACRO ANGLE

(A) INTRODUCTION AND WIDER ISSUES

After ten years of reform, we do not have much to boast of by way of the desired impact. What is particularly deplorable is that there is no widespread threat perception yet. The fear of loss of jobs has not emerged significantly enough to boost efficiency allround. While trade unions are objecting to reform specifically on the ground that workers will be thrown out of factories and offices, this is not out of a sense of fear. In fact, they are confident that they and those whom they seek to protect will be able to hold their own. Yet, a feeling of job insecurity is a key aspect of an ideal form of liberalisation and on this depends the growth of competitive spirit. Workers necessarily must feel unsure of their jobs and pay pockets and, likewise, managers must be in a state of suspense about what will happen to them in the coming days. There is no justification, under a truly liberal environment, for a personnel perception that demonstrates no worry over the future. Any identification with *status quo* runs counter to the reform spirit. The protected market, over long years, had safeguarded needless jobs along with inefficient producers. This is precisely what should be sought to be replaced by a truly competitive regime under a process of liberalisation, which, ostensibly was the prime goal of the various measures initiated in mid-1991.

Admittedly, in the financial sector, mutual funds as well as other financial service companies have had to yield to market compulsions. While they went on a recruitment spree with extravagant pay packets thrown in when the going was good, they did not hesitate to respond to a crisis by way of drastic job and wage cuts. But, such dynamism has eluded public sector banks. There, trade unions have refused to show any flexibility. Time and again, they have bargained hard for pay hikes and against any form of rationalisation of the work force. While pursuit of a firm course of liberalisation would have demanded tough action on staff-related matters — much more than what was recommended by the M.S. Verma working group on restructuring of weak public sector banks — the unions remain stuck to their traditional tactics and have refused to even inch towards a personnel policy that would make the banking sector more and more combative in global terms.

RESTRUCTURING OF SICK BANKS

Consistent with its terms of reference, the working group constituted by RBI in February 1999 was determined to rise to the challenges of financial sector reform, at least in regard to public sector banking entities that were losing heavily. Its report submitted to the Reserve Bank in October 1999, more or less, set the initial agenda for a performance-oriented banking system.

The working group's strategy for revival of the ailing constituents of the public sector segment of the nation's banking system was broadly as follows:

- Seven parameters were to be applied, these pertained to three key areas: (I) Solvency (capital adequacy ratio and coverage ratio), (II) Earning capacity (return on assets and net interest margin) and (III) Profitability (ratio of operating profit to average working funds, ratio of cost to income and ratio of staff cost to net interest income + all other income).

- The definitions/tests provided by the Committee on Banking Sector Reforms (CBSR) should be supplemented by a performance analysis based on the seven parameters cited above for identifying areas of weakness in banks in future.
- The seven parameters could also be used to evolve benchmarks for a competitive level of performance by public sector banks; to begin with, these benchmarks could be set at the median levels of ratios pertaining to the 24 public sector banks (excluding the three identified weak banks, viz. Indian Bank, UCO Bank and United Bank of India).
- Narrow banking could not by itself be adopted as a long-term restructuring strategy.
- Closure involved many negative externalities affecting depositors, borrowers and employees and should not be exercised unless all other options were exhausted.
- A comprehensive restructuring could succeed, but called for firm and decisive actions in the exercise of hard options. The Government, management and employee unions must agree upon every important condition of the proposed restructuring programme before its launch.
- Restructuring of weak banks should be a two-stage operation, stage one involving a process of operational, organisational and financial restructuring aimed at restoring competitive efficiency and stage two covering options of privatisation and/or merger.
- Operational restructuring essentially involved building up capabilities to launch new products, attract new customers, improve credit culture, secure higher fee-based earnings, sell off foreign branches (Indian Bank and UCO Bank) to prospective buyers

including other public sector banks, pull out from subsidiaries (Indian Bank), to establish a common networking and processing facility in the field of technology, etc.

- The action programme for handling of non-performing assets (NPAs) should cover honouring of Government guarantees, better use of compromises for reduction of NPAs based on the recommendations of the settlement advisory committees, transfer of NPAs to the Asset Reconstruction Fund (ARF) managed by an independent Asset Management Company (AMC), etc.
- To begin with, ARF could restrict itself to the NPAs of the three identified weak banks; the funds needed for ARF were to be provided by the Government; and ARF should focus on the relatively larger NPAs (Rs.50 lakh and above).
- A 30-35 per cent reduction in staff cost should be undertaken in the three identified weak banks to enable them to reach the median level of ratio of staff cost to operating income.
- In order to control the staff cost, the three identified weak banks should adopt a voluntary retirement scheme (VRS) covering at least 25 per cent of staff strength; for the three banks taken together, the estimated cost of VRS ranged from Rs.1,100 to Rs.1,200 crore.
- The organisational restructuring included delaying of the decision making process relating to credit, rationalisation of branch network, etc.
- Financial restructuring involved efforts to maintain a capital adequacy ratio (CAR) well above the minimum required level, a further recapitalisation subject to strict conditionalities relating to operational

and organisational restructuring of the recipient bank, etc.

- System restructuring to include setting up of an independent agency under a special act of Parliament to approve bank-specific restructuring programmes, initiate their implementation and monitor their progress. Such an agency to be designated as the Financial Restructuring Authority (FRA).
- The existing legal provisions, which were out of line with the present day realities, needed to be amended and new enactments relating to bankruptcy, foreclosures, etc. made.

For speeding up the recovery process, a mechanism should be worked out to make the debt recovery tribunals (DRTs) more effective.

BEYOND SICK CONSTITUENTS

Significantly, the Verma working group did not stop with the three identified sick players and declared itself on other public sector banks as well. Indeed, on the basis of all its seven operational parameters, only three banks were operating wholly on a sound basis. While several others failed to meet many of the norms set by the working group, some like the Syndicate Bank just about escaped being listed among the sick because of certain fortuitous factors. Obviously, the working group did not want any of the banks to assume that they could manage as they had been doing all along. This message should get across to the staff unions as much as those managing the various banks in the country, in the public as well as private sector.

While the working group was asked by the Reserve Bank to confine itself only to the public sector segment, the IMT study is focussed on the entire banking system. This is warranted all the more by the fact that in respect of private

TABLE – I

Working Results of Scheduled Commercial Banks (SCBs) for 1997-98 and 1998-99

	SBI GROUP		*19 Nationalised Banks*		*27 public Sector Banks*		*Foreign Banks*		*25 Old Pvt. Sector Banks*		*9 New Pvt. Sector Banks*		*All SCBs*	
	1997-98	*1998-99*	*1997-98*	*1998-99*	*1997-98*	*1998-99*	*1997-98*	*1998-99*	*1997-98*	*1998-99*	*1997-98*	*1998-99*	*1997-98*	*1998-99*
A. Rupees Crore														
A. Income	24871	29349	42835	49518	67706	78867	8697	9719	6438	7361	3015	4131	85857	100078
i) Interest	21209	25126	37867	44348	59076	69474	6783	7857	5496	6498	2395	3541	73751	87370
ii) Other Income	3662	4223	4968	5170	8630	9393	1914	1862	942	863	680	590	12106	12708
B. Expenditure	22412	27884	40265	47725	62677	75609	8068	9026	5996	7050	2616	3733	79354	95418
i) Interest Expended	13904	16983	26269	30857	40174	47840	4222	5201	4084	5088	1820	2777	50299	60905
ii) Intermediation cost	6235	7719	11025	12731	17259	20450	1931	2579	1272	1482	456	669	20917	25180
iii) Provisions and Contingencies	2273	3182	2971	4137	5244	7319	1915	1246	640	480	340	287	8138	9333
C. Operating Profit	4732	4648	5541	5929	10274	10578	2545	1940	1082	791	740	684	14640	13992
D. Net Profit	2460	1466	2570	1792	5030	3528	630	693	443	311	400	397	6502	4660
E. Total Assets	232843	285904	416661	484417	649504	770321	65098	76623	54966	65423	25845	38531	795412	950898

(Contd...)

	B. Per Cent of Total Assets													
A. Income	10.68	10.27	10.28	10.22	10.42	10.24	13.36	12.68	11.71	11.25	11.9	10.72	10.79	10.52
i) Interest Income	9.11	8.79	9.09	9.15	9.10	9.02	10.42	10.25	10.00	9.93	9.27	9.19	9.27	9.19
ii) Other Income	1.57	1.48	1.19	1.07	1.33	1.22	2.94	2.43	1.71	1.32	2.63	1.53	1.52	1.34
B. Expenditure	9.63	9.75	9.66	9.85	9.65	9.82	12.39	11.78	10.91	10.78	10.12	9.69	9.98	10.03
i) Interest Expended	5.97	5.94	6.30	6.37	6.19	6.21	6.49	6.79	7.43	7.78	7.04	7.21	6.32	6.40
ii) Intermediation cost	2.68	2.70	2.65	2.63	2.66	2.65	2.97	3.37	2.31	2.27	1.76	1.74	2.63	2.65
iii) Provisions and Contingencies	0.98	1.11	0.71	0.85	0.81	0.95	2.94	1.63	1.16	0.73	1.32	0.74	1.02	0.98
C. Operating Profit	2.03	1.63	1.33	1.22	1.58	1.37	3.91	2.53	1.97	1.21	2.86	1.78	1.84	1.47
D. Net Profit	1.06	0.51	0.62	0.37	0.77	0.42	0.97	0.90	0.81	0.48	1.55	1.03	0.82	0.49

Note: Number of foreign banks for 1997-98 and 1998-99 are 42 and 44 respectively.
Number of scheduled commercial banks for 1997-98 and 1998-99 are 103 and 105 respectively.

sector banks the proportion of the provision adjusted or net non-performing assets (NPAs) to total assets rose from 2.3 per cent as on March 31, 1998 to 2.9 per cent as on March 31, 1999. In an earlier study by IMT, "*Industry & Business: Ethics and Accountability*", reference was made to a serious act of fraudulence involving a New Delhi branch of the Vijaya Bank, which had been rated the best among private sector banks prior to its nationalisation. Surely, it cannot be that fraudulence surfaced only after that entity came under public ownership and control and had been free from an abuse of such nature as long as it was privately managed.

The idea is not to mock at the reform effort in the financial sector, but only to address the managerial challenges in the area of banking objectively and not subjectively. Yet, one must concede that these challenges are considerably more daunting in the public sector than in the private sector. One obvious reason for this is the dominance of public sector undertakings (PSUs). The total assets of 27 public sector banks were Rs.770,321 crore during financial year 1998-99 as against Rs. 76,623 crore of foreign banks, Rs. 65,423 crore of 25 old private sector banks and Rs. 38,531 crore of nine new private sector banks. But, an important factor is that the public sector segment has less flexibility on matters of staff and management and operational practices, duly reflected in a lower operating profits to assets ratio compared to that of the foreign banks and the nine new entities in the private sector.

STRENGTHENING THE SYSTEM

Yet, it must be accepted that in order to strengthen the financial system, a procedurual attempt has been made in stages since 1991 to move towards full disclosure, transparency and effective supervision of banking operations in line with practices rated to be the best internationally. With effect from the accounting year ending March 2000, banks were advised by the Reserve Bank of India to disclose in the "Notes to

Accounts" additional information on (a) the maturity pattern of (I) loans and advances, (II) investment in securities, (III) deposits and (IV) borrowings, (b) foreign currency assets and liabilities, (c) movements in NPA and (d) lending to sensitive sectors like real estate, capital market and other sectors as defined by the RBI from time to time.

In view of the growing share of investments in the assets of banks, the RBI decided to extend the risk weight of 2.5 per cent for investment in approved securities to all investments, including non-SLR securities with effect from March 31, 2001. It further lowered the exposure ceiling in respect of an individual borrower from the earlier level of 25 per cent to 20 per cent of banks' capital funds with effect from April 1, 2000. Where the existing level of exposure as on October 31, 1999 was more than 20 per cent, banks are required to reduce the exposure to 20 per cent of the capital funds over a two year period (by end-October, 2001). A Reserve Bank working group under Mr. Jagdish Capoor, Deputy Governor, reviewed the existing system of deposit insurance with regard to deposits of coverage, institutions to be brought under insurance cover, etc. The working group suggested no change in the present deposit insurance coverage (Rs. 100,000 per depositor), but recommended a limited co-insurance for deposits between Rs.90,000 and Rs.1 lakh.

PROFITS AND PROVISIONS

The profitability analysis of scheduled commercial banks (SCBs) revealed a decline in profits during 1998-99 (Tables I & II). A substantial increase in provisions and contingencies by nearly 40 per cent over the previous year led to a significant decline in the net profits of public sector banks. Despite a fairly significant decline in provisions and contingencies, the net profits of private sector banks also declined in 1998-99. In the case of foreign banks, the decline in provisions and contingencies contributed to higher net profits in 1998-99. For

SCBs as a whole, provisions and contingencies increased by about 15 per cent and this contributed to a decline of 28.3 per cent in their net profits. The operating profits of SCBs declined by 4.4 per cent from Rs.14,640 crore in 1997-98 to Rs.13,992 crore in 1998-99. As can be seen from Table II, the operating profits of all bank groups except the public sector banks declined in 1997-98. Even in the case of public sector banks, the operating profits of the State Bank of India (SBI) and its associates registered a marginal decline of about two per cent. The operating profits of nationalised banks, however, increased by seven per cent in 1998-99.

TABLE II

Variations in Profits of SCBs (1998-99)

(Rs. Crore)

Banking Group	*Operating Profit*	*Provisions and Contingencies*	*Net Profit*
1. Public Sector (i +ii)	303.8 (3.0)	2075.4 (39.6)	-1771.6 (35.2)
(i) SBI & Associates	-84.3 (-1.8)	909.8 (40.0)	-994.1 (-40.4)
(ii) Nationalised Banks	388.1 (7.0)	1165.5 (39.2)	-777.5 (-30.3)
2. Private (Old)	-1.4 (-26.9)	-159.7 (-25.0)	-131.7 (-29.8)
3. Private (New)	-55.3 (-7.5)	-52.8 (-15.5)	-2.5 (-0.6)
4. Foreign	-604.9 (-23.8)	-668.3 (-34.9)	63.4 (10.1)
Total	-647.8 (-4.4)	1194.5 (14.7)	-1842.3 (-28.3)

Note: Figures in brackets show percentage change over the previous year.

There have been changes in the net profit structure of various bank groups on account of increase in competition as well as diversification of activities. The share of State Bank of India and its seven associated banks (SBI Group) increased from 19.3 per cent of total net profits to SCBs in 1991-92 to 31.5 per cent in 1998-99, while the share of nationalised banks declined from 43.9 per cent to 38.5 per cent during this period.

The share of foreign banks in the total net profit of SCBs also declined from 30.4 per cent to 14.9 per cent, whereas the combined share of old and new private sector banks increased from 6.4 per cent to 15.2 per cent during the same period.

NET INTEREST INCOME (SPREAD)

The net interest income or spread of nationalised banks registered a marginal increase from 2.78 per cent of their total assets in 1997-98 to 2.79 per cent in 1998-99. However, the corresponding proportion in respect of the SBI Group declined by 29 basis points from 3.14 per cent to 2.85 per cent during the same period. As a consequence, the net interest income of public sector banks, which account for more than 80 per cent of the total business of SCBs, declined by 10 basis points from 2.91 per cent of total assets in 1997-98 to 2.81 per cent in 1998-99. During this period, the net interest income of old private sector banks declined by 41 basis points from 2.57 per cent of their total assets to 2.16 per cent, while in the case of new private sector banks it declined by 25 basis points from 2.23 per cent of total assets to 1.98 per cent in the same period. As regards foreign banks, the net interest income declined by 46 basis points from 3.93 per cent of their total assets in 1997-98 to 3.47 per cent in 1998-99. Nevertheless, it is significant that of the different bank groups the foreign banks group registered the maximum spread in 1998-99 at 3.47 per cent, followed by the SBI group at 2.85 per cent, nationalised banks at 2.79 per cent, old private sector banks at 2.16 per cent and the new private sector banks at 1.98 per cent as against the average of 2.78 per cent for all SCBs.

NON-PERFORMING ADVANCES

A non-performing asset in India represents an advance that has not been serviced, as a result of "past dues" accumulating for 180 days and over. A distinction is also made in India between gross and net NPAs. In view of the time lag in the recovery process and the detailed procedures and safeguards involved in regard to write-off, even after making provisions for advances considered irrecoverable, banks continue to hold such advances in their books. These are termed gross NPAs while provision-adjusted NPAs are termed net NPAs. The net NPAs of SCBs declined marginally from three per cent of their total assets as on March 31, 1998 to 2.9 per cent as on March 31, 1999. The corresponding proportion in respect of public sector banks declined from 3.3 per cent to 3.1 per cent while it increased from 2.3 per cent to 2.8 per cent in respect of private sector banks during the same period. In the case of foreign banks, net NPAs declined from one per cent of their total assets as on March 31, 1998 to 0.8 per cent as on March 31, 1999. As the build-up of NPAs has been a major factor in the erosion of profitability of public sector banks in India, the Narasimham Committee had underscored the need to reduce the average level of net NPAs for all banks to three per cent by 2002. The definitions of weak banks given by the Committee have refined the concept of NPA.

The Verma working group on restructuring of weak public sector banks supplemented the above definitions by a combination of seven parameters covering solvency, earnings capacity and profitability. The high level of NPAs of banks in India reflects the weak loan recovery mechanism. Data as on March 31, 1999 indicate that out of the total number of 21,781 cases involving a sum of Rs. 17,921 crore transferred to or filed with the debt recovery tribunals (DRTs), the number of cases decided was 3,774 or 17.3 per cent of the total and these accounted for ten per cent of the total locked-up amount in the cases transferred to or filed with DRTs. The net NPAs of SCBs as a whole increased marginally from 7.3 per cent of their net advances in 1997-98 to 7.5 per cent in 1998-99.

The net NPAs of public sector banks declined marginally from 8.2 per cent to 8.1 per cent, whereas those of private sector entities increased significantly from 5.3 per cent to 6.9 per cent during the same period. The net NPAs of foreign banks declined from 2.2 per cent in 1997-98 to 2.0 per cent in 1998-99. The gross NPAs of all SCBs (sub-standard + doubtful + loss) increased from 14.4 per cent of their gross advances in 1997-98 to 14.6 per cent in 1998-99 (Table III). As regards different bank groups, the gross NPAs of public sector banks declined marginally from 16.0 per cent to 15.9 per cent while the gross NPAs of private sector banks increased significantly from 8.7 per cent to 10.4 per cent during the same period. The gross NPAs of foreign banks also rose from 6.4 per cent to 7.0 per cent in this period.

TABLE – III
Classification of Loan Assets of SCBs
(percentage distribution of total loan assets)

Assets	*Public Sector*	*Private*	*Foreign*	*All SCBs*
Standard				
1997-98	84.0	91.3	92.5	85.6
1998-99	84.1	89.6	93.0	85.4
Sub-standard				
1997-98	5.1	4.8	3.9	4.9
1998-99	4.9	6.0	3.6	4.9
Doubtful				
1997-98	9.1	2.9	0.8	7.7
1998-99	9.0	3.6	1.5	7.8
Loss				
1997-98	1.9	1.0	1.7	1.8
1998-99	2.0	0.9	1.9	1.9
Total				
1997-98	100.0	100.0	100.0	100.0
(Rs. Crore)	(284971)	(36753)	(30972)	(352696)
1998-99	100.0	100.0	100.0	100.0
(Rs. Crore)	325328	(44492)	(31433)	(401253)

CAPITAL ADEQUACY

The capital to risk-weighted assets ratio (CRAR) reflects the financial viability of commercial banks. As on March 31, 1999, the CRAR of public sector banks as a whole was 11.2 per cent, which was marginally lower than the level of 11.5 per cent attained as on March 31, 1998. However, all public sector banks except one have achieved a CRAR of nine per cent as on March 31, 1999. As per the prudential norms set, SCBs were required to achieve a CRAR of nine per cent by March 31, 2000 and this requirement has been generally met. A number of banks entered the capital market to satisfy the capital adequacy norm. Till end-March, 1999, eight public sector banks raised capital through equity issues from the new issues market. More of them did likewise in the subsequent period. In fact, the Government has been encouraging public sector banks to raise capital through public issues. To facilitate this, they have been allowed to write off the accumulated losses against the paid-up capital, so as to enable them to have higher earnings per share. The growing presence of commercial banks in the capital market was reflected in the increase in number of banks listed on the recognised stock exchanges from six SCBs in 1994-95 to 28 SCBs in 1998-99. As at end-March, 1999, the shares of eight public sector banks and 17 private sector banks were listed for secondary market trading on the National Stock Exchange (NSE). Others followed suit later on.

BANK SUPERVISION AND REGULATION

The term of the Board for Financial Supervision (BFS) in the RBI, which is the supervisory authority for banks, all-India financial institutions (AIFIs) and non-banking financial companies (NBFCs), was extended upto March 27,2000. The main supervisory issues addressed by BFS related to on-site and off-site supervision of banks, AIFIs and NBFCs and the registration and prudential norms of NBFCs. The on-site supervision system for banks is on an annual cycle and is based on the 'CAMELS' model. It focuses on core assessments in accordance with the statutory mandate, i.e., solvency, liquidity, operational soundness and management prudence. Banks are rated on the basis of this assessment.

In view of the recent trends towards financial integration, globalisation and technological upgradation, it has become necessary for supervisors to supplement on-site supervision with off-site surveillance. The aim is to capture early warning signals from off-site monitoring, which would help avert a financial crisis of the East Asian or Latin American magnitude. The off-site monitoring system consists of returns on capital adequacy, asset quality, large credit and concentration, connected lending, earnings and risk exposures (viz., currency, liquidity and interest rate risks). These efforts are further supplemented by an in-depth analysis of the secondary market movements of listed scrips, which serve as an indicator of public confidence in the financial performance of banks. In order to enable banks to manage the risks associated with asset-liability mismatches, detailed guidelines on asset-liability management and risk management systems have been issued by RBI. The RBI also strengthened sometime ago the existing supervisory framework in India in relation to the BASEL core principles, which represent the minimum essential requirements for effective banking supervision as laid down by the BASEL Committee on Banking Supervision. These principles are spelt out in detail later on. Steps are being taken to bridge the gaps, which are mainly in the area of risk management, consolidated supervision, inter-agency cooperation and cross border supervision. But, all these measures have been largely procedural in nature and their impact on managerial and staff attitudes has been minimal.

SECTORAL DEPLOYMENT OF BANK CREDIT

The details of sectoral deployment of bank credit may be seen from Table IV. During 1998-99, out of the total increase in non-food gross bank credit amounting to Rs.37,398 crore, 40.4 per cent flowed to priority sectors comprising agriculture,

TABLE – IV

Sectoral Deployment of Gross Bank Credit Variations during[1]

Items			April-October				April-October	
	1997-98	*1998-99*	*1998-99*	*1999-2000*	*1997-98*	*1998-99*	*1998-99*	*1999-2000*
			(Rs. Crore)				*(per cent)*	
I. Gross bank credit	41292	41729	12638	18589	15.9	13.9	4.2	5.4
1. Public food procurement	4888	4331	4243	4588	64.3	34.7	34.0	27.3
2. Gross non-food credit	36404	37398	8395	14001	14.5	13.0	2.9	4.3
(a) Priority sector (i+ii+iii)	14627	15104	3924	5678	17.2	15.2	3.9	5.0
(i) Agriculture	3427	4765	1750	1536	10.9	13.7	5.0	3.9
(ii) Small scale industry	7564	4975	592	174	21.0	11.4	1.4	0.4
(iii) Other priority sectors	3636	5364	1582	3698	21.5	25.4	7.5	15.0
(b) Medium and large industries	14926	12986	2293	1981	10.3	11.0	2.0	1.5
c) Wholesale trade (excluding food procurement)	877	748	-61	1247	3.0	5.7	-0.5	8.9
(d) Other sectors	5974	8560	2239	5095	18.0	14.9	3.9	7.7
II. Export credit[2]	3939	1944	-1056	-1800	1.4	5.7	-3.1	-5.0

1. As on the last reporting Friday of the period.
2. Also included in non-food credit; figures in the paragraph on export credit are more up-to-date.

Note : Data are provisional and relate to 50 scheduled commercial banks, which account for 90-95 per cent of the bank credit of all scheduled commercial banks. Gross bank credit data include bills rediscounted with RBI, IDBI, Exim Bank and other approved financial institutions.

small scale industries and other priority sectors while 34.7 per cent flowed to industry (medium and large). The sectoral break-up of credit for the period April-October, 1999-2000 showed an increase of five per cent in priority sector credit compared with 3.9 per cent in the corresponding period of the previous year. Credit to large and medium industries increased at a lower rate — by 1.5 per cent — during that period than the two per cent achieved in the corresponding period of 1998-99. Credit to wholesale trade increased by 8.9 per cent as against a decline of 0.5 per cent in 1998-99. However, export credit dropped by five per cent during April-October 1999-2000 as against 3.1 per cent in the same period of 1998-99.

EXPORT CREDIT

Banks are required to lend 12 per cent of their net bank credit to the export sector. The outstanding export credit of SCBs at Rs. 36,827 crore as on March 26, 1999 represented an increase of Rs. 2,397 crore or seven per cent over the outstanding credit of Rs. 34,430 crore as on March 27, 1998. As on December 3, 1999, the outstanding export credit amounted to Rs. 38,136 crore, an increase of Rs. 3,263 crore or 9.4 per cent over the same period of the previous financial year. During 1999-2000, the export credit refinance limit of SCBs increased *vis-à-vis* last year and stood at Rs. 8,651 crore as on December 3, 1999. The average utilisation of export credit refinance ranged from 46.9 per cent to 82.5 per cent of the refinance limit during April-November, 1999. With effect from April 1, 1999, export credit refinance is provided to SCBs at the bank rate.

PRIORITY SECTOR CREDIT

The priority sector advances of SCBs (as per provisional data) increased by Rs. 5,678 crore or five per cent during April-October 1999 as against Rs. 3,924 crore or 3.9 per cent in the comparable months of the previous financial year. About 70 per cent of the incremental advances to the priority sector during April-October 1999 flowed to the category "other priority sectors" in contrast to 40 per cent in 1998-99. Priority sector advances by public sector banks rose to 43.5 per cent of net bank credit (NBC) as on the last reporting Friday of March 1999 from 41.8 per cent of NBC. Advances to the agricultural sector from public sector banks in 1998-99 constituted 16.3 per cent of NBC while the proportion in respect of the SSI sector was 17.3 per cent. Priority sector advances of private sector banks increased from 40.9 per cent of NBC as on the last reporting Friday of March 1998 to 41.4 per cent of NBC as at end-March 1999. In their case, advances to agriculture constituted 9.5 per cent of NBC, while those to the SSI sector accounted for 18.9 per cent. The foreign banks, for whom the priority sector lending target is 32 per cent of NBC, also registered a significant increase in priority sector advances to 34.3 per cent as at end-March, 1999. Their advances to the export sector accounted for 25 per cent of NBC as at end-March 1999 while the SSI sector received 11 per cent of net bank credit.

RURAL CREDIT

Though rural financial institutions have played a leading role in the provision of rural credit, the rural sector, especially the agricultural sector, according to the Union Finance Ministry, is still in need of more credit. The National Bank for Agricultural and Rural Development (NABARD), the apex organisation in the field of rural credit, has taken several initiatives in this regard. Notable developments in recent years have been the introduction of Kisan Credit Card (KCC) and the linkage of self-help groups (SHGs) with banks. Against the target of 20 lakh KCCs in the Union Budget for 1999-2000, the issue of KCCs by the public sector banks in the country numbered 9.1 lakh during April-December 1999. The amount sanctioned through these cards was Rs. 2,377 crore, which worked out to Rs. 26,161 per card. In order to enable NABARD to leverage its capital funds for raising more resources, its capital base has been progressively increased from Rs.500 crore in 1996-97 (at the rate of Rs.100 crore by the Government of India and Rs.

400 crore by RBI every year) to Rs. 2000 crore as on March 31, 1999. Besides share capital contribution, the Reserve Bank has been providing to NABARD a general line of credit (GLC) under Section 17(4E) of the RBI Act to enable it to meet the short term credit requirements of co-operatives and regional rural banks (RRBs). A line of credit of Rs. 5,700 crore (Rs. 4,850 crore under GLC-I and Rs.850 crore under GLC-II) was sanctioned to NABARD for the year 1999-2000 (July-June). An additional limit of Rs. 400 crore under GLC-I was given in December 1999.

An important development in the area of rural infrastructure has been the creation of the Rural Infrastructure Development Fund (RIDF) in 1995-96 under NABARD, with a corpus of Rs. 2,000 crore, to provide funds to State Governments and State-owned corporations to enable them to complete various types of rural infrastructure projects. So far, there have been five RIDFs (RIDF-I to RIDF-V) with a total corpus of Rs. 13,500 crore. The funds for RIDF are mobilised from domestic commercial banks on the basis of the shortfall in their priority sector advances *vis-à-vis* the stipulated targets. The cumulative sanctions and disbursements out of RIDF amounted to Rs. 12,109.33 crore and Rs. 4,639.48 crore respectively as at the end of November 1999. An analysis of the trends in utilisation of RIDF at the state level has revealed a substantial shortfall *vis-à-vis* sanctions. There have, however, been inter-state variations in this regard. In some States, the utilisation has been poor mainly due to inadequacy of their own funds to supplement the provisions under RIDF. Elsewhere, there have been other factors. In order to enable the States to enhance utilisation, the Union Budget for 1999-2000 widened the scope of RIDF to include lending to Gram Panchayats, self-help groups and other eligible institutions for implementing rural infrastructure projects.

NO REFORM SPIRIT YET

Banking, unfortunately, has seen very little of the reform

spirit in the decade that has gone by, in terms of staff attitudes and perceptions. Managers and subordinates are what they are and have been, although the Reserve Bank of India has, for its part, demonstrated its policy preparedness for internationally competitive banking. Measures have been taken, albeit with some caution, to make the banking and other segments of the financial sector perform increasingly in a global environment. But, this policy intent has been neutralised by a largely bureaucratic administration and a staff force that simply refuses to move with the times. Those on the pay roll, whether they be of the officer cadre or belong to the multitude of clerks and other file pushers, are determined to do no more them just stick around. This was the traditional rule of a regime that, obviously, was a mockery of the market place. This mockery remains and, what is worse, nobody is willing to see it as one. The powerful unions want no change. They must have the periodical wage revisions, and other related or unrelated benefits, but without any noticeable improvement in productivity. Indeed, intransigence against the essentially reformist cuts in wages and jobs is their answer to demands for truly commercial banking.

The Narasimham Committee's words of wisdom have been met with nothing but deafening silence. Anyone familiar with the ways of the so-called nationalised banks know that nothing will change. There is no fear of the deadwood among staff being asked to wind up and to go home. Everyone around is so sure of his/her job and the monthly pay packet — with the bonus and pay revisions thrown in — that the customer will have to wait to be served, that too only indifferently. It is a miracle that cheques get cleared and amounts debited and credited in this age of anti-reformist sluggishness and lethargy. This is no unfair indictment, but only a brutal statement of the appalling facts on the ground. There are as a rule more people than what a branch needs and can afford to keep. As for computers, there are more of them in different stages of repair or should one call it hibernation? The one entrusted with an essentially mechanical function of pass book entries remains inoperative for days together and it is a mercy that after a fortnight someone sets it right. It is another matter that the computer goes back to sleep after a while and a note is put up for depositors to avoid troubling the person in charge with inconvenient queries about the entries.

SMALL MERCIES

Indeed, most of us are quite happy with the small mercies and do not think that the service must be faster and more efficient. We are all prepared to solicit favours from the officer and the clerk and to thank them profusely for services that they are paid to render, that too much too generously. When will banks address the very basic issue of mounting overheads? The Rangarajan Committee had set the agenda quite some years ago for computerisation of banking activity. Bank managements had then agreed under pressure from the militant unions not to hurt the staff in any form. This agreement still holds and computers have not displaced anyone. The software companies are getting a lot of business from banks allright, to the point where bank staff conveniently gets disoriented when these companies choose to play truant. Banks hold up payments so as to put pressure on the systems engineers and the latter settle scores by not servicing the computers they have put in place. The software outfits have mushromed because of banks' ineptness and are in a position to harass bank branches all the more as the staff here does not bother to learn enough of the systems to be able to do without the software engineers in regular attendance. No doubt, it is in the interest of the software companies to keep banks underprepared for the challenges of full-scale computerisation. They are careful not to give their customers the kind of programmes, which would cut into their own business. But then, this is just what anyone in their position will do. It is for banks to enhance their level of computer literacy.

Yet, computers are only a peripheral aspect of the anarchy that is the sad story of the Indian public sector banking segment. Generally, there is no sense of urgency whatsoever, and everyone is basking under the knowledge that the unions are there to safeguard the interests of staff and promote the well being of managers and supervisors alike. The latter can build as many flats as they want and no embarrassing questions are asked about an employee seeking the bank's financial support for having more than one flat. The children can be sent abroad for higher studies, with generous support from the employing banks, under a staff welfare scheme. Several consumer durables can be acquired with concessional bank loans. This extravagant package will remain, reform or no reform. The only difficulty that the staff faces is that while officers can be posted outside a state every three years clerks must be prepared for being moved from place to place within a state. This part of the service hurts allright, but then, when we consider all the benefits this is only a small price to pay, which the staff should not really mind.

MEANER AND LEANER

Banks have to become meaner and leaner. On this, I must offer a clarification. Everyone of us having something to do with bank personnel might have justification to feel that they could not get any meaner in terms of their lack of professionalism generally and a work life that openly declares apathy to efficient service and innovativeness, meaning those characteristics that are not of the fraudulent variety. The words 'leaner and meaner' are intended to convey the message that banks should not offer any free lunches and should get more — not less — out of any transaction. Fraudulence is not even faintly suggested. Nor is it held out that customers should be increasingly harassed in the name of their becoming more and more commercially oriented. A commercial orientation should have as an aspect a mix of probity and customer-friendly service. This demands underscoring in the present context. While long years of forced involvement in efforts to promote public interest, obviously, led to a wanton neglect of professionalism and also helped foster fraudulence, this must cease to be offered as an impediment to growth of truly professional commercialisation.

The staff may want to be perpetually tied to the past in regard to the approach to its service conditions and benefits, but then, banks presently — and even earlier — have a role different from yielding readily to the dictates of the politician. This role has got to be assumed at least now with a sense of urgency. Ten years after the Indian economy was formally put on the reform path, no excuses can be offered for the continued pursuit of a financial regime that is the anti-thesis of efficiency. True, the world over, banks, time and again, still have to succumb to the power of the State and even in the United States banking entities have perforce to serve State policy in terms of preferred credit. Yet, the World Bank had rightly taken the stand that populist operational pursuits ran counter to the commercial banking sector's fundamental goals. While the Bank's annual *World Development Report* consistently objected to Indian priority sector lending, this had not been singled out for adverse comment and generally the Bank did not take kindly to populism displacing the very basic commercial character of banking activity worldwide. If the Gramin Bank experiment in neighbouring Bangladesh had, indeed, won international acclaim, this was only because this innovation designed to meet the needs of the economically and socially under-privileged sections of the community rested firmly on the premise of prudent banking — a premise that has consistently eluded the Indian efforts to take banking to the poor and downtrodden. Several things are, no doubt, wrong with the Bangladesh economy and polity, but the Gramin Bank part of the nation's development strategy remains a solid demonstration of banking as it should be practised in any country, regardless of its political and social-economic constraints.

DICTATING UNIONS

Policymakers have a role in that they should have stopped,

as early as in 1991, treating the segment owned by the Government as a departmental undertaking. Unfortunately, even as late as 2000 this process has not begun. The unions continue to decide the parameters of reform and the Government lets them do so. This is a sad commentary on the progress towards liberalisation. The Union Finance Minister cannot still muster the courage to tell the Indian Banks Association to begin dictating to the unions. The Association is forced to accept what the unions want and North Block, rather, uses liberalisation to deny the Association the support it badly needs to begin dictating to the staff and officers unions. If the Indian Banks Association cannot flex its muscles, it is entirely pointless for it to be around. We cannot, obviously, have a ceremonial body in a critical sector as banking. In any case, a reforming banking sector cannot have a common decision making process. Each bank, whether it is privately owned or owned by Government, must negotiate with its own workers and managers and follow operational as well as staff policies largely on its own. The parameters laid down by the Verma working group have to be viewed as among the scientific means of deciding a bank's policy and other reflexes. Lending and deposit rates apart, everything that a bank management does or does not do must be in response to its specific circumstances. Obviously, those banks meeting all the seven parameters cannot be asked to fall in line with those that are barely surviving and *vice versa.* Likewise, what is admissible to the latter cannot be thrust on the former. Since 1991, there has been a lot of loose talk about banks being allowed to pursue a course of their own, but this has largely remained an exercise in rhetoric and everyone continues to believe in the safety of numbers.

The good performers must exercise the best options, while the laggards must have survival as their immediate goal. In their choice of options, neither the RBI nor the Indian Banks Association should have any say and banks must pursue measures that are in their own interests. While anarchy is hardly suggested, those who run a bank must freely do what they perceive to be good for it and not venture on something simply because someone in the North Block, the PMO or elsewhere believes that it will work. Banks, should have, a decade ago, taken upon themselves — without any pressure from outside — the tasks of sound commercial entities. It is not too late in the day to ask themselves whether they can come up to international standards. Knowingly, they missed the bus. Now, they just do not know how fast they can make up for lost time. It is not an easy world for anyone to do business in and things are only getting harder. The South East Asian crisis only added to the problems of risk management. The bitter memories of the 1991-92 securities scandal, which involved a number of banks, and the irregularities that surfaced in the Indian Bank are a serious impediment to any strategy that would put the banking sector on a reforming path. For, reforms essentially demand doing away with the cushions of the past. Transparency over non-performing assets calls for the best in risk management. For a sector that has all this long relied on papering over cracks, risk management poses a daunting challenge. The capital adequacy ratio, provisioning, prudential norms and a close monitoring of NPAs are part of the essential efforts to push Indian banks into the global banking mainstream. For entities that have survived largely by pushing things under the carpet, these constitute a tough globalisation agenda. But, there is simply no escape from this and bank managements have to break away from the illusory comforts of the past. The various 1991-92 acts of securities-related fraudulence had exposed brutally the banks' proclivity to manipulating their transactions. If as the key player in all this, Mr. Harshad Mehta, suggested then, most transactions would have been squared up in the normal course, then, obviously, bank managers were taking recourse to book keeping practices that bordered on the reckless. Such recklessness, clearly, should not be demonstrated in the present context of a growing demand for prudence and pursuit of sound practices. Banking constituents, regardless of who owns them, have got to be dynamic without losing sight of their bread and butter and their bottom line.

STATE-DICTATED BANKING

Banks necessarily have to be more competitive than industry, business and service providers, which, unfortunately, nobody realises. One must acknowledge that the spirit of competitiveness has not become pervasive in these segments. Yet, liberalisation is generally seen to be addressed to the non-financial sectors. No doubt, the Narasimha Rao Government had wasted no time in setting a reform agenda for the financial sector through the Narasimham Committee. But, the common perception has consistently been that the non-financial corporate sector should lead the way in preparing the economy for the demands of globalisation. This could be partly on account of the recognition that the banking activity in particular would continue to be largely State-dictated and driven. This itself could have been prompted by the fact that much of the agenda set by the Narasimham Committee has remained untouched. Indeed, it is this standstill which has provided the justification to IMT's eighth study.

Several factors have contributed to the slow pace of financial sector reform. Primarily, the State needed the support of banks to meet its responsibilities towards the community at large. While banks as well as non-banking financial entities were expected to have a commercial stake in the financing of development activities in business, industry and the services sectors, such a stake was not considered feasible in respect of development in other areas. Since the interests of agriculture and rural development continued to be advanced mainly through State patronage and only residually through private initiative, banks could not get out of the old regulatory orbit and could not say yes to suggestions that they must sacrifice public interest in the pursuit of a commercial orientation. This explained why foreign, private and public sector banks all have social commitments thrust on them and have to meet on a preferential basis the credit needs of sectors that were designated as priority areas more than twenty years ago. Effectively, for banks the twenty point programme of the late Mrs. Indira Gandhi continues to be the gospel, reform or no reform. It is a mercy that a particularly ugly aspect of the programme — loan melas — do not torment bank officials any longer. It may be recalled that under a protege of Mrs. Gandhi — Mr. Janardhan Poojari — the melas had acquired a particularly vicious character. In contrast, in industry, private initiative and profit motive are encouraged as part of a process of liberalisation and several areas that were no entry zones for private entrepreneurs have been thrown open to them. The public sector industry, no doubt, goes without an agenda, but this has not come in the way of private industrial houses expanding their sphere of influence and in the process making it harder still for public sector undertakings to do business.

A LOUD PROCLAMATION

It is clear that the staff unions are taking advantage of the State's pivotal role in socio-economic development and the fact that banks have to play a major part in rural development and farm sector growth. The staff knows that banks can never acquire a total commercial orientation because of these commitments and that this constraint will also come in the way of any serious effort towards privatisation. Yet, when we consider that neither banks nor other financial entities can keep — or can be kept — out of the global mainstream indefinitely, nobody should make the developmental compulsions an excuse — much less a justification — for the perpetuation of a regime of blackmail by the trade unions in the banking sector. Banks have no rationale for postponing true reform on the ground of social obligations. In fact, one aspect of the Verma working group's assessment of public sector banks — the fact that a few banks have been able to meet all the seven performance-related parameters — loudly proclaims that a good performer can meet the social burden and still come out on top. Nothing, in fact, can be a deterrent to a bank with a strong commitment to professional functioning. While this can be no case for complacency among the constituents with a good track record, yet this achievement is not to be dismissed lightly.

Ideally, of course, preferential and concessional lending must get phased out and banks must finance rural development and farm sector growth strictly on the basis of true commercial merit. Interest subsidies and preferential credit facilities have to be done away with and whosoever is in need of bank finance must seek it less on the strength of political or other clout and more on the basis of viability. Poverty alleviation is essentially the State's responsibility. Rightly, the Narasimham Committee had mooted a time-bound reduction in priority sector lending, although neither this nor the proposal for a substantial cut in the statutory liquidity ratio has received the desired administrative response. For farm loans to acquire a commercial dimension, it is important that every farm-related activity should be market-oriented and should cease to survive on the basis of bribes and open or disguised protection. Instead of looking up to the Government to raise the prices of various crops season after season, farmers should produce competitively and sell commodities within as well as abroad that win buyers on the power of superior quality and real economic price.

FARMS AND BANKS

The WTO regime may fail to force the Indian farming community into this free market environment because of the protection it offers by way of a formal acknowledgement of the necessity for a massive public distribution system. Obviously, Indian policy makers have to go well beyond the WTO diktat to push growers of various commodities into the true market place that is largely free of the Government and of the administrative machinery. They have to do this rather than take refuge under the WTO shelter. They must, in the process, in fact, risk the prospect of farmers not helping to sustain the public distribution system and choosing instead to go to the free market. The transition from a PDS-led farming activity to one driven by the pulls and pressures of the free market is a major step towards bringing the farm sector within the ambit of reform. It is this, which will really facilitate the banking sector's acquisition of a strong commercial orientation. Initiatives for this necessarily have to come from the political leadership and administrative machinery. As for the banks themselves, their own role will necessarily have to be restricted to minimising the impact of interest and credit subsidies on their bottom line. The success that some constituents of the public sector segment have achieved, as per the assessment of the Verma working group, has to be emulated by all the lesser performers and that too within a specific time frame.

This is, no doubt, a challenge, but ducking this is hardly the best way of going about the matter. We can all want to live perpetually in the past, believing in the illusory wisdom of wishes being horses. But, the fact is that wishes rarely become horses, unless these are backed by a sincere and painstaking effort. Bank managements and staff should have realised quite sometime ago that they had a big battle on their hands. They have to fight and not back away. The CEOs must stop assuming that they are placed no differently from the corporate czars and letting their ego - duly reflected in opulent offices - cloud their perspectives about strategies. Instead of using the entire floor area quite wastefully to give an affluent and luxurious look, the big bosses of public sector banks must begin doing their work — and more of it — from smaller and more businesslike chambers. What really matters is their combative performance and not luxury. They have to sell their products at the least cost and make big gains year after year and month after month. To start with, they must rent out much of the area used for the CMD's office.

RECALLING KEATS

Keats wrote of marriage as an exercise in misery for

women and not bliss as was widely and conveniently assumed. Banks for their part have long been inflicting a condition bordering on misery on its customers. The former Union Finance Minster, Mr. T. T. Krishnamachari had mistakenly believed — and spread this belief — that debtors dictated to the banks and the latter were free to take lightly the depositors, the creditors. But, under long years of public ownership, only the bank staff has been calling the shots, whether it be in respect of those who needed the banks' financial support or those who put their funds with the banks. Keats knew what was coming to the dreamy young women who saw in a marital state a life of perennial joy. Such realism eluded the political radicals of the late sixties, who deceived themselves into thinking that with nationalisation banks would meet public interest better than in the past. The consequence has been that in the name of public interest creditors and debtors alike were given a shabby treatment. Reform, ideally, should have made banks truly customer-friendly. But, a decade of reformist initiatives by the Government and the Reserve Bank of India has gone by with staff insensitivity towards customers' interests only growing and not weakening, as it should have.

This is effectively proving Keats only dead right, albeit to a scenario that least concerned him. The English poet may otherwise be quite irrelevant to all those who sit in various counters and handle ledgers. For them, the only poetry that makes sense is the hike in pay and other payments that they bargain for every time this comes up for upward revision. Nothing else matters to them. Basically, attitudes have refused to change. Everyone who matters in the banking system wants to go on as if nothing has changed. No reform if this means tightening the screws on them - this is the tune that bank unions are determined to play in defence of those whose interests they claim to represent. For bank employees, their marriage with the various debtors and creditors should only work to their own benefit. People and institutions should patronise them so that they can give themselves more pay and other benefits. On their own part, the managers and other staff would exploit or oblige the borrowers and lenders so as to ensure that their own interests are served better. The various irregularities that surface or get pushed under the carpet are some reflection of the game of general exploitation or selective patronage that is played day in and day out. Those singled out for preferred treatment may be anybody — it may be a stockbroker one day, an influential politician another day or an industrialist with clout some other time. This is the true economics of the Indian banking market place. The massive magnitude of the reported scandals should easily explain the nexus between bank officials and persons in other spheres with connections. It only seems fair that where fraudulence is established and punishment meted out the ones to bear the consequences of a wanton neglect of professionalism and rectitude are more often the bank officials and not always their partners in crime. The bank staff has, in the wake of the 1991-92 securities scandal, sought to protect itself by persuading the Union Finance Ministry to accept their contention that banking frauds and irregularities should not be indiscriminately entrusted to the CBI for investigation. But then, the CBI is hardly inclined to go soft on bank frauds. I am returning to this later, particularly to call for a balanced approach to the issue.

ACCEPTING CHANGE

Banks should know that they have a specific job to do in an environment of change. Primarily, they have to accept the wisdom of change. In fact, it is that reluctance to do this which is to blame for the total want of unpreparedness on the part of all but a few public sector banking entities to take up the challenges of globalisation. Departmental attitudes have to change as much as those of other institutions. Indeed, private businesses have also got to accept that they cannot forever operate in a protected environment. While the *sarkari babu* and the politician must realise that they aren't here any more to dictate and to collect bribes, the private entrepreneur must likewise learn to do business without perpetually having to move the Government and the administrative machinery.

Yes, things are hardly reassuring on this count. For, when a populist Union Communications Minister decides to give free phone connections to all telecom employees who, oddly enough, are part of a corporate entity since October 1, 2000 — leaving the Prime Minister with no option but to endorse his decision — he sends a strong message across that for him reform does not matter at all. The access to any facility except on a commercial payment is anti-reform and the free market operates on the basis that every product or service has to be paid for and will never be available *gratis*. The bank unions are, thus, in good company. The Supreme Court has, no doubt, ruled decisively against any effort to render a mockery of the principle of natural justice by endorsing the dismissal of an indisciplined employee of the Syndicate Bank. The bank unions cannot, obviously, do anything against such a sensible and timely ruling, but they can still refuse to accept the wider message that is part of the ruling. Bank managers and staff do not have to do anything sensible when they have people like the Communications Minister and the leftists, who are against any substantive reform of the banking sector, on their side. But, the fact is that the reform spirit has to spread in the banking sector and quickly. Banks have failed to change in the first decade of liberalisation, but this hardly means that the second decade should go the way the first has gone.

THE TRAGEDY THAT IS

The tragedy of Indian banking is that it is not even ready to accept the necessity of reform. It wants to keep everything, that has contributed to its total lack of commercial character, in tact. The quality of management overall is such that few would be prepared to accept without any reservations the operational excellence of a few public sector entities that the Verma working group has highlighted. Just as the Syndicate

Bank escaped being classified as a sick unit by the working group because of certain dubious aspects of its operations, the best of the lot might have also benefited from some helpful factors that lay outside the working group's ambit and duly escaped its attention. This could be the perception of critics of the report.

After all, not everyone is agreed that the Verma working group's report is the last word on the efficiency or otherwise of the public sector component of the nation's banking system. Indeed, serious doubts have been voiced over the group's approach and the wisdom of the conclusions it reached. What, however, goes to the group's credit is that it spoke up strongly against the intransigence of bank staff generally and for giving banking policy and practice a substantial measure of professionalism. But, that does not still mean that in respect of a competitive reform of the banking sector the various facts highlighted in the report are significant enough to constitute the broad agenda. At best, the report should be seen as the first, but certainly not the last word.

In fact, the initiatives towards making Indian banks global performers over a period should be harsher and be more comprehensive than what the working group was prepared to accept. The public sector as well as other banks must be subjected to a closer scrutiny and their deficiencies at the branch — not just at the overall bank — level identified and urgent corrective action initiated. This scrutiny much go well beyond the statutory audit and the special checks prompted as much by crises as by serious allegations. Checks need to be made concurrent and not *post mortem*. The reform to make banking activity in the country truly competitive in global terms must cover all aspects and can ill afford to be piecemeal or whimsical. There can be no room for populism in any area of banking activity. Economies must be real, not notional, and the impetus for these, ideally, should come from the staff itself. Efficiency levels are certain to go up significantly if performance ceases to be contrived and instead is driven by true fundamentals. Basically, all banks must spend less and less and earn more and more. Banks have little choice, as far as the future is concerned, between closures and shedding their flab.

BANKS MUST DIVERSIFY

Perhaps, just as industrial houses can freely get into financial activity banks should also be allowed entry into non-banking activity, if for nothing at least to fruitfully absorb the staff rendered surplus because of reform. Banks should have the freedom to do what they perceive to be to their maximum advantage, even to the point of going slow on their main activity and giving more importance to other areas. After all, under reform when there is no objection to industrial corporates setting up financial subsidiaries there can be no harm in banks being asked to take up business not related to banking. I am saying this in earnest and not in jest. In fact, the staff must begin to think on these lines. Managers and subordinates have long been tied to a notional promotion of public interest and to a bureaucratic style of functioning. Now, they must be able to visualise a dramatic change in the scenario that includes their being told to handle a business that they have not done all this long. I believe that unions must be actively involved in the process of change for the better, which effectively means the staff being entrusted with non-traditional functions. Deadwood, wherever it is, will never accept any transformation, but then, the unions must stop being the protectors of those workers and managers who have no business to be around.

The unions must get into forefront of the effort to faster professionalism. They must willingly do this, instead of being pushed into this. If jobs have to be kept, this must be done through efficiency leading to larger business and meaningful diversification of activity. The union leaders have long pursued a dog-in-the manger policy. It is high time they ditched this approach in favour of a truly dynamic one. I would gladly take on this note, though I had begun as an uncompromising critic of unionised banking. Ultimately, what this critical segment of the nation's economy achieves will depend on how its managers and staff perform. The unions have consistently decided the level and quality of performance, which hitherto meant only keeping the jobs in tact with an ever rising remuneration. Now, they have to play a different tune, which they can do provided they apply themselves to the task.

A DIFFERENT ROLE FOR UNIONS

Banking was an activity that should never have been entrusted to those with a laid-back attitude to life. After all, no loan can be advanced casually and without checks and cross checks of the borrower's creditworthiness. With all kinds of pressure being brought on them, managers at the branch as much as at other levels rarely had an easy time. They had to avoid making a mistake about the safety of a loan and getting too closely involved with any borrower. They were required to know that any unholy nexus would hurt them ultimately when the balloon burst. Now, the unions have to make the ground safer for professionals by resisting pressure on behalf of the branch level managers and those elsewhere. Their priorities have to shift from those of standing up for the deadwood and for indiscipline to making professionalism the watchword.

The approach to VRS and the policy decision by the Government on disinvestment of 33.3 per cent of its equity holding in public sector banks, in diverse ways through, constitute an agenda for professionalisation of banking activity in the country. But, neither is the real remedy to the present lethargy. The staff response to the VRS offer has been quite warm —in terms of the reduction in jobs and wage-related costs — but the cost of VRS itself is considerable. The Government is moving the World Bank for support, and justifiably in so far as the scheme is a key aspect of financial sector reform. But, individual banks have to bear the cost impact. Mr. Kohli has dealt with the matter comprehensively in his introduction. The Union Budget for 2001-02 has, for its part, added a new dimension to staff management by dispensing with the banking services selection board and leaving the respective bank managements to take care of selection in conformity with their requirements.

(B) PRACTICES Vs COMPULSIONS

Practices in any sector cannot let themselves be dictated largely by compulsions. Surrendering to pressures or constraints does not make for a sound policy or procedure. In banking, the world over, however, this golden rule has been breached often to the point where infringements have been increasingly treated as the rule rather than the ugly exception as these should be. Indeed, if only those running this crucial segment of economic activity had accepted judicious operation as the very basis of their performance, then the monitors and watchdogs within and outside the system could have afforded to take their own functions lightly. The Bank for International Settlements (BIS) might well have been reduced to an ornamental agency if every bank manager went strictly by the copybook. There would have no global debt crisis of the magnitude that had erupted in August 1982, and the BIS would not have been shaken so rudely as to force on the commercial banking system overall tough prudential norms and render a stringent level of capital adequacy a key aspect of banking policy and operations in various countries.

Central banks in different countries would be breathing easily but for Governments on the one hand thrusting their own fiscal burdens on banks and the latter in turn seeking to neutralise the strains and stresses arising out of a glaringly expedient transfer of these burdens by doing a lot of things that prudence ideally should warn against. In a significant pronouncement of banking policy and practice — the M. G. Kutty memorial lecture delivered in 1993 by then Reserve Bank Governor, Dr. C. Rangarajan — it was emphasised that the autonomy of central banks held the key to pursuit of a healthy monetary policy. On that basis, a strong demand was voiced for marginalising Central Government access to Reserve Bank credit and also making it incumbent on the government sector to pay the market rate of interest to banks on the resource support provided by the latter by way of investments in Government and approved securities. Reference was made to the authority wielded by the Federal Reserve in the United States and the Bundesbank in Germany. The Union Finance Ministry responded firmly to the specific proposals on reduced Central recourse to RBI's kitty and payment of market-determined rates of interest to banks for their investments in Government securities.

ELUDING BASIC ISSUES

But, the basic issues in the development of banking on a sound commercial basis have remained unaddressed. These pertain to the social or public interest priorities of the banking sector. The M G Kutty memorial lecture's thrust was so much on Central bank autonomy that the pressures of statutory lending ratio and priority sector lending on commercial banks did not receive the attention due. The Narasimham Committee, no doubt, called for a phased reduction in the statutory liquidity ratio as well as the level of priority sector lending. The ratio itself has been cut, but certainly not to the point where the Reserve Bank's consistent grievance in the past — of the commercial banks' lendable resources being pre-empted by the demands of Government funding — was fully taken care of.

One obvious explanation for the massiveness of the 1991-92 securities scandal was the fact that while commercial banks necessarily had to subscribe to the bond issues of Central and State Governments and organisations owned by them the return on these instruments was so low as to become a big liability on the banking system overall. Banks willingly played into the hands of brokers in a situation where there was no regular secondary market for all the securities that they were saddled with. The Union Finance Minister of the time, Dr.

Manmohan Singh, duly acknowledged that the yields on the securities were low and that there was no market for these instruments. He also spoke of a systems failure to explain away the gravity of the crisis.

But, the basic question was much deeper than what the magnitude of fraudulence had raised. Frauds were no doubt committed and there was a manipulation of accounts on a truly gigantic scale, but what really emerged was that there was simply no commercial rationale in the policy of compelling banks to invest in securities that were simply unsaleable.

INEVITABILITY OF FRAUDS?

Yet, the question asks itself why only some banks were involved in the scandal and not all of them. The involvement of foreign banks was explained by the fact that they were the ones, which were actively trading in Government securities. This raised an important issue — apparently while these banks had no difficulty finding secondary buyers for the low-yielding securities the ugly fact that emerged was that they needed to be party to frauds for making the sale itself possible. They were no doubt booking losses, but surely this was not the best way of attracting secondary buyers. Coming to the banks which were not part of the scandal, obviously, the losses that they were incurring they were either absorbing or showing these in the balance sheets. If these were less than what resulted from the kind of irregularities that constituted the scandal, then, obviously, these were both ethically and commercially justifiable, not merely defensible.

Banks, essentially, have to borrow cheap and lend dear and pocket the gains. But, this is easier said than done since lendable funds have to be lured to banks in preference to so many other investment options that are open to depositors. This cannot be done with offers of returns that are not competitive. This compulsion rules out the idea of borrowing cheap. Banks cannot also lend dear in a macro situation where costly credit is perceived to be anti-growth and where, as the major lenders, they are required to assist diverse segments of the economy and, obviously, they cannot be doing this with a Shylock-like approach. This compulsion on banking entities is duly reflected in a narrow spread between borrowing and lending rates. The seven parameters used by the Verma Committee for different public sector banks have to be seen in this light. Where all these are met, the spread turns out to be commercially very sound, not just manageable. Yet, we can very well see that this is the ideal — obviously not generally, achievable — economics of the banking market place.

As the committee's report showed, with only three exceptions, none of the public sector entities had performed on a commercially satisfactory basis. This was a sad commentary on the quality of management in the public sector segment of banking. Unless we know for certain that banks in the private sector are generally faring much better and doing so without being unethical, we cannot offer privatisation — assuming that this course is acceptable to the unions — as a strategy for the commercial viability of PSUs in banking.

COMPULSIONS SHOULD'NT DICTATE

Yet, there is a strong case against compulsions — strictly operational as well as extraneous — being offered as a policy package and requiring bank managements to toe the line as dictated by these compulsions. Banks must do what they ought to as their set functions require them to do, and not either less or more. This basic norm did not become sacrosanct merely because of liberalisation and should have been consistently honoured even in the long years of public ownership and control under a regime of regulation. Nationalisation did not necessarily have to be accompanied by a chaotic situation, one that we still encounter 30 years after the event, which itself had been wildly applauded as a great act of economic and political radicalism then and for many years thereafter.

The Government's take-over of the supposedly best run banks and those with the largest assets did not have to be characterised either by a wilful neglect of financial management or an indiscriminate and totally unwarranted addition to manpower year after year. Public ownership did not have to be widely seen as a licence for inefficiency at all levels and in all positions. Nobody could lay down that with the Government as the owner there could be many more workers in offices than was commercially justified. A total commercialisation, indeed, ought to mean a high level of professionalism and freedom from the kind of pressures and pulls that are operationally and otherwise unwarranted. This has to be well understood. Prudential norms, whether in regard to assets and liabilities or manpower, necessarily have to be honoured — and not certainly in the breach — and no excuses could be offered in this respect.

Quite clearly, neither governments nor the unions can lay down the ground rules. The compulsion that any bank management can or should justifiably yield to is profitability. Of course, long term gains should matter more than temporary benefits. Shortsightedness should be averted always and as a matter of course, and not by fits and starts. Banks should cease to have social goals that are inconsistent with enhanced profitability. This is not to say that U. S. based banks were justified in financing cocaine-related deals or that the foreign banks operating in India were being perfectly legitimate in colluding with fraudulent stock brokers in the months leading to the 1991-92 massive securities scandal. Profit making even under an extreme form of liberalisation should not ever get equated with fraudulence in any form or of any magnitude.

While on this, the point must be made, however, that a bank official's capacity or proclivity for corruption should not be exaggerated. The staff transfer policy which often borders on lunacy ostensibly has this pious policy — discouraging corrupt tendencies. Favours are certainly shown on caste, linguistic and other personal considerations and the requirement of transfers after three years' service for bank officers is known to be selectively relaxed in respect of the favoured officials. Why this policy at all? Why not minimise staff movement from one place to another and keep the same person in the same place and even take care to see that promotions are given in the same city? The important issue is why equate corruption with continuity in service in one branch for a period longer than three years. This equation is quite senseless knowing that bigger acts of fraudlence have been traced to members of the top brass, who did not come under the ambit of the staff transfer policy.

In the course of my lecture on *Frauds in Government securities* delivered at the CBI Academy on August 10, 2000, predictably, the issue of criminal intent came up. This is fundamental to establishing responsibility for any act of fraudulence. I took the view that the actions of bank officials should be evaluated on the basis of the circumstances bearing on the transactions carried out. I warned against a standard law and order approach that was determined to see a fraudulent motive behind even a perfectly realistic response to a specific — obviously, a difficult — market situation. I acknowledged that frauds — meaning transactions that could be established as such — were taking place but, I noted that bank officials at different levels were constantly under pressure from various quarters. My view was that it could be less than fair to make a retrospective evaluation of the sanctions given for fresh loans or enhancement of existing credit limits at an earlier point of time.

'Subsequently, I had several rounds of discussions with senior bank managers on the kind of pressures under which they had to function. Retrospective judgements are among the hazards of banking operatons. While generally the findings of inspections are time-barred, with three years being the cut-off point, there are times when officials not in favour are sought to be 'fixed' with managements wilfully neglecting the time bar as part of this selectively vindictive exercise. Such victimisation happened in respect of a former chairman of a leading bank, who had made the mistake of not doing his PR work with the required diligence. His aloofness generally — this functionary was said to have had minimal contacts even at high level meetings convened by the RBI Governor — led to his being acutely embarrassed shortly before his retirement with a vindictive inquiry into a petty deal involving him. If the CEO of a large public sector bank could be harassed in this manner — even while several of his counterparts elsewhere with shady transactions behind them got away as very honourable people — one can imagine the lot of smaller men and women trying to make an honest living out of an environment that was often taxing. Given its statutory requirements, the CBI, cannot, obviously, be expected to take note of the role of political or other connections in evaluating the integrity or the lack of it on the part of bank officials. Yet, it is not fair to condemn some people or vindicate some others on the basis of the absence or presence of powerful godfathers.

STICKY LOANS AND NPAS

On the critical issue of responsibility fixing for sticky loans and non-performing assets, obviously, professionalism demands an objective measurement of the role played by sanctioning managers. While as per procedure sanctions are required to be given only after a close look at the fundamentals concerning borrowers and a thorough monitoring, including stock audits by outside agencies, is provided for, a situation leading to defaults in interest payments often emerges to the embarassment of managers who initially decided the creditworthness of borrowers. Also, despite the elaborate procedure, there are times when the lack of creditworthiness of borrowing companies is overlooked because of collusion between the latter and the concerned bank officials. Oral instructions continue to be given to subordinate officials and the latter are forced to sanction loans that, left to themselves, they would not have done. Sometime ago, despite the known and acknowledged fact that a leading public sector bank had an exemplary record of over 90 per cent of its loans being fully secured, one of its prestigious branches in Maharashtra was forced to report a substantial NPA merely because its biggest account failed. Admittedly, NPAs and the level of security are not related. NPAs depend on the recovery of the loans provided and not merely on how secured the latter are. Nevertheless, this particular development can hardly be excused. There was, obviously, an unholy collusion, which did not reflect very well on the quality of bank management.

Recovery is crucially linked to the performance of the borrower and only later on to the security of the loans given. Also, security does not automatically mean that the overdue amount can be realised fully and swiftly. The Government has, no doubt, strengthened the debt recovery process, but recovery itself is still a time consuming matter. No wonder, the Government has allowed bank managements to go for compromise or write off. Clearly, the best run bank would use these courses only minimally.

Here, it must be understood that loans continue to be the highest profit-earning assets for banks. The general consensus among bank oficials at the senior level is that there will be no change in this even under a deepening process of liberalisation. Since non-fund business is generally linked to credit expansion, it implies that in order to earn fee-based income also, banks will have to rely more and more on credit. Though with reform there have been suggestions that banks should go for non-traditional risk-taking avenues such as derivatives, securitisation and financial advisory services, obviously, until such a time that the financial markets assume considerable maturity and sophistication, lending will remain a core business of banking and the risk associated with credit will constitute the most significant one facing banks. The precision with which the credit risk can be evaluated affects not only the profitability of loans given but also the extent of rejection of requests for loans that might have proved unprofitable to the lenders. This explains why banks have to continually search for better and surer ways to assess the credit risk.

EVALUATING CREDIT QUALITY

The credit appraisal system in Indian banks has come a long way from the time an advance was given against pledge of securities and has served to meet the need-based requirements of different classes of borrowers. Yet, traditionally, credit appraisal involves looking at the 5Cs (character, capacity, capital, collateral and conditions) or 4Ms (man, machine, material and market). The emphasis, broadly, has been on identifying two factors viz. the intention or willingness to repay and the capacity to repay. While the intention itself involves a close scrutiny of the credentials of borrowers for ascertaining the level of integrity, the capacity to repay is assessed on the basis of various financial analyses. Guidelines for such areas as assessment of credit needs, fixing the level of holding of inventory and receivables by industrial borrowers, calculating the magnitude of permissible bank finance and for the interest rate chargeable have been issued from time to time by RBI. For large advances, banks were required to seek credit authorisation from RBI and the Credit Authorisation Scheme (CAS), over the years, became some kind of a regulatory syndrome. The situation has, however, changed with liberalisation and banks now are free to formulate their own guidelines on many of these matters. Even so, the attitude generally is one of feeling safe with RBI's diktat and otherwise expecting the Indian Banks Association to lead. The freedom that one associates with liberalisation is not surfacing, though one supposes that managers must be prepared for acting on their own at least five years from now, if not sooner. True reform demands such dynamism, though, obviously, this cannot develop with an attitude outside that rewards a safety-first worklife and punishes initiative.

Now, turning to credit rating, this is being increasingly used as a risk management technique. In the developed countries, more and more banks, for quite some years now, have been grading their loans very much like what the rating agencies have been doing in respect of various financial instruments. The rating process is a useful exercise at the time of credit appraisal as well as at the monitoring stage. In the appraisal stage, the rating process brings greater precision to a lending decision. In addition, by rating the customer first and then evaluating the proposed facility, the process helps in deciding the loan covenants or other non-price terms.

A PRIMITIVE REGIME

However, the credit rating system in the Indian context is somewhat primitive and is used only for the sake of pricing of risk rather than, as it should be, being developed into a risk measurement system. The mechanism of credit rating in the nationalised banks themselves lays considerable emphasis on the conduct of various accounts followed by different financial parameters. The conduct of account mainly covers timely submission of stock statements, quarterly information system (QIS) and renewal data, compliance with inventory norms, the regularity or otherwise of the account, the average utilisation of the limits in the account and adherence to repayment schedules. The financial parameters mainly consist of the current ratio and the debt equity ratio. Too much stress on the current ratio without the managements bothering to go into its composition and also having a standard benchmark for the debt-equity ratio as well as the debt service coverage ratio (DSCR) without taking into account the industry profile may fail to serve the desired purpose. Banks have got to move away from a glaringly unscientific practice of pricing a risk based on the perception of the customer to one based on the technical assessment of the risk involved while ensuring transparency. Factors, which reflect the risk of default, must get considerable weight. Therefore, factors relating to industry risk, business risk and management risk have to be incorporated in the rating process. Indeed, banks have to think in terms of limiting the rating of a specific firm to the overall industry rating, somewhat on the lines of the internationally accepted mode of restricting the individual rating to the sovereign rating.

In the course of business, banks grant various credit facilities, and as long as the conduct of the account is proper and regular, there is no obvious strain on the lender. But, the moment the account goes irregular, for whatever reason it may be, panic sets in. No wonder, when credit facilities are sanctioned, the borrower and other parties execute loaning, security and other documents which detail the arrangements including repayment and various other rights of the creditor, in the event of default by the liable parties. Banks also obtain balance and security confirmation letters from the borrower/ guarantor from time to time. The balance and security confirmation letter is, in essence, a reminder to the parties about the "debt". In fact, the liable party acknowledges this "debt" and the bank sends a statement of account, which effectively is a communication conveying that the balance runs into debit and the party is indebted. When an account either goes irregular or comes to a standstill, the concerned bank managers/officials approach borrowers informing them of the banks' concern and persuading them to maintain requisite financial discipline. Banks formally make a request in writing, asking the liable parties to regularise the account.

AN ELABORATE PROCESS

If persuasion and follow-up fail, then legal action is considered. As a preliminary to the legal proceeding and in order to warn the liable party that the matter will reach the court of law, a legal notice (though not a must) through a counsel is given. The notice also cautions that the liable party would be liable to pay all costs. This effectively gives another opportunity to the liable party to remedy the situation. If the notice fails to evoke any response, then the necessary steps for initiating legal proceedings are taken. Legal proceedings may take various forms. These may vary in relation to the amount due, the forum in which the proceedings are to be initiated, the relief intended to be provided and the special remedies available under the statute.

The process runs as follows:

(a) Suit in court

(b) Certificate proceeding

(Application before the Debt Recovery Tribunal (DRT))

(c) Reference to BIFR

(d) Application for winding up of the borrowing enterprise.

(e) Reference fcr arbitration, wherever applicable.

Whatever be the type of legal proceeding, initially a notice/summon is sent making known to the defaulter that the bank has initiated statutory action and requires a reply or written statement in response. On the liable party's appearance before the appropriate authority, the matter is further adjudicated. In case the party fails to put in an appearance, the matter is decided unilaterally. Ultimately, the court/tribunal/forum passes a decree/order confirming the right of the bank to recover the amount from the liable party. The bank in question then takes the necessary steps to execute the decree/order/certificate in the manner prescribed under the law.

From the stage of execution of the loan documents — which, by itself, casts an obligation on the liable party to pay the debt as per the repayment arrangement specified in the document and every other follow-up measure — "demand" is the essence of every effort to ensure recovery. There is no justification either to feel shy or shirk responsibility in making the "demand". "To demand" is not only a matter of "right" of the creditor (banker) but also one of remedy (legal proceeding).

There is an old proverb that goes somewhat like this:

"Without timely watering, no crops will grow.

Without regular practice, no art will be perfect.

Without safety measures, what you have will not remain with you.

Without a firm demand, no loan will be repaid."

NARASIMHAM COMMITTEE'S SUGGESTIONS

On a suggestion from the Narasimham Committee, debt recovery tribunals have been set up and presently there are ten of them. But, their record in recovery of bad debts of banks has been lackluster. This is regrettable. Banks being derivative institutions, their well-being or otherwise is inextricably linked to the other sectors of the economy. Therefore, bank losses are ultimately borne by the economy and the loss allocation has serious policy connotations. If we take the amount of recapitalisation of banks which is presently of the order of over Rs 20,000 crore from budgetary sources, then the loss has been mainly borne by the taxpayers. The Narasimham Committee reiterated its proposal for the formation of ARCs and made a strong case against further bank recapitalisation. But, while recapitalisation is not only costly and in the long run also unsustainable, the ARCs are not also the panacea to the problem of bad debts. The Narasimham Committee suggested the hard-core NPAs of most banks being carved out and transferred to an ARC, which could be funded and manned by the banks themselves so as to maintain "institutional memory" on NPAs to effect recoveries. The Committee further recommended securitisation of such loans and establishment of ARCs by banks and DFIs as well as appropriate changes in the legal system and provision of tax incentives. Obviously, a lot of ground work needs to be done before the problem of NPAs can be effectively tackled through ARCs. The experience of state financial corporations (SFCs) in the recovery of their dues holds out a warning against undue optimism. Despite being empowered to take possession of assets as well as arrange for their sale under Sections 29, 31 and 32 of the SFCs Act, 1951 and a reasonably expeditious settlement of cases by the courts, the NPAs of SFCs are uniformly much higher than those of banks. There is really nothing like a one shot resolution of the problem.

Both in theory and practice there are two aspects of NPAs: stock and flow. These are by no means unrelated. How to ensure that banks do not generate high levels of new NPAs after a carve-out of NPAs at any one point of time is essentially a question of addressing the "flow" aspect. If the backlog of NPAs represents the "stock" aspect, "flow" losses arise from the making of fresh loans, which turn bad. The "flow" problem is best addressed by tackling the underlying causes for loans turning bad i.e., the real sector losses. There is an inextricable link between financial and real sectors and the former's health is largely a reflection of the latter's performance. It must be remembered that in many of the southern cone countries the decline in real economic growth during the eighties had resulted in a very high level of NPAs and eventually provoked grave banking crises. Addressing the NPAs issue will be meaningful only if this exercise is coupled with a drastic restructuring of the real sector whereby unviable firms are forced to exit.

CREDIT RISK RATING

Credit risk rating is the pivot around which the various functions of a bank's credit department are bound.

This has the following aspects:

a) ***To lend or not***: Within the rating framework banks are required to decide the rating beyond which they will not take any additional exposure. Rating helps in deciding the rating/ grade upto which accepting additional exposure can be considered.

b) ***Pricing***: Borrowers with a weak financial position and placed under the high credit risk category should be priced high. Banks should evolve scientific systems to price the credit risk, which should have a bearing on the expected probability of default. The pricing of loans should be linked to risk rating. However, factors such as value of collateral, market forces, the perceived value of accounts, future business potential and strategic reasons may also play an important role in pricing.

c) ***Norms for collateral/margins***: The extent of collateral security required and the need to step up margin requirements are linked to the credit risk rating of a borrower. The higher the risk category is the higher will be the volume of collateral required and the margins stipulated. Banks have to evolve appropriate norms on the above aspect.

d) ***Product mix guidelines***: There is an imperative need to shift totally away from borrowers availing of the credit facility by way of the cash credit limit to term lending in working capital. In case of the high credit risk category, banks may consider offering demand loans for a shorter duration keeping in view the risks involved. Similarly, for borrowers in the low credit risk category the banks may consider fixing the line of credit/pre-sanctioned limits for disbursal at short notice. Similarly, a declining cash credit rate based on the volume of credit that may be availed of by low risk category borrowers also has to considered.

d) ***Delegation of powers***: The delegation of loaning powers may be linked to the credit risk rating of a borrower. Managers at various levels have to apply their expertise in evaluating exposure to high credit risk category borrowers rather than high volume borrowers only. Similarly, the delegation of loaning authority should also be linked to the maturity of the loan.

e) ***Vary the frequency of renewal and follow up-process***: Renewal of the loan facility in case of the low credit risk category of borrowers can be considered biannually whereas for high risk rating borrowers this can be done twice a year or even at quarterly intervals.

PROCESS OF CONSOLIDATION

The process of consolidation in the banking industry has got off to a brisk start with the announcement of acquisition of the Times Bank by the HDFC. The market responded warmly to the move by registering a 40 per cent increase in HDFC's stock. The merger gives the HDFC over 650,000 retail accounts, a network of 107 branches, deposits of Rs 7,000 crore and a total balance sheet touching Rs. 10,000 crore, making it the leader among private and foreign banks. In terms of size, the HDFC has a combined staff strength of 1115 (660 of HDFC + 455 of Times Bank). While personnel is not expected to be an area of cost savings, in others there is obviously scope for cost reduction, considering that the merged entity can switch to a single V-SAT system connecting all the branches. The merger also enhances the scope for cross-selling and rightly, the strengthened entity offers everything from loans and mortgages to mutual funds, debit cards and insurance.

Driven essentially by a concern for survival, consolidation can spread faster in the private banks segment. Clearly, size is critical to these banks and mergers between the new and old entities could prove beneficial to both. For the new private banks, mergers should confer the advantage of a vastly improved branch network, while the older constituents stand to gain in terms of technology. The number of private banks in the country might shrink significantly in the coming years. The new private sector banks are also planning to get into insurance. The acquisition of Computer Age Management Services (CAMS), a registrar and transfer agent, by the HDFC Bank is expected to help the latter in its insurance business.

As regards the public sector segment, the bigger constituents may lack the urge for mergers as they already enjoy the advantage of size. However, when disinvestment of Government equity in public sector banks gains pace, the process of consolidation might force itself on the smaller nationalised banks, which might want to merge to acquire the clout that goes with size. It is also possible that some of the non-banking institutions might get a substantial stake in public sector banks. The UTI has already indicated that it would acquire a nationalised bank once the Government sheds its equity significantly. Since the Government does not favour cross-holding between banks and Fls, consolidation through mergers seems a distinct possibility.

As the financial markets integrate and acquire a significant level of maturity and the debt market also develops strongly, the result will be a process of disintermediation and this will hurt banks. This could also provide a fillip to consolidation and, eventually, we may see a banking structure almost similar to what was suggested by the Narasimham Committee viz., a few large banks with an international presence and some smaller banks catering to specific geographical areas. But, in that eventuality the term 'bank' will cease to connote what has traditionally been understood i.e., accepting deposits for lending. The new millennium bank could well be a one-stop financial shop.

(C) PUNJAB NATIONAL BANK: A REVIEW

OPERATIONAL PERFORMANCE

During the year ended March 31, 2000, the Punjab National Bank adopted various strategies to improve its profit ability. While most of the available opportunities for augmenting revenues were utilised, the Bank focussed on enhancing its holding of low cost deposits. Reduction in NPAs, particularly the mid-cap segment, also came under sharper focus. In order to achieve an improved risk dispersal and to utilise the large potential in the personal banking segment, the management initiated a major drive in financing consumer durables, professionals and self-employed persons and traders. Even as housing finance was stepped up, lending for agriculture was also accelerated. Steps were taken to popularise PNB Krishi Cards, an avenue that is aimed at the farming community. In order to improve generally the quality of service to customers, the Bank adopted the ISO-9000 quality management systems standards. During the year, a number of divisions were covered under this quality movement. Adoption of such standards is deemed important particularly as competition grows and choices widen and enlarging the customer base is possible only with better and more efficient service. The main goal of the quality movement is to draw closer towards the customer. This policy initiative has already resulted in an improved ambience in many of the branches and investments in computerisation.

The operating profit of the Bank at Rs. 820.16 crore during 1999-2000 was marginally higher than the previous year's Rs. 821.27 crore. This modest rise was mainly because of the payment/provision of Rs. 96 crore towards wage revision for the officers and workmen of the Bank and the procedural changes in calculation of interest on term deposits (multi-benefit scheme). The Bank, however, earned a net profit of Rs. 408.14 crore during the year compared to Rs. 372.12 crore in 1998-99, registering a growth of 9.7 per cent.

CREDIT MANAGEMENT

The advances of the Bank registered a growth of Rs.3,525 crore or 18.5 per cent over end March 1999 to reach a level of Rs. 22,572 crore at the end of March, 2000. The loan policy retained its emphasis on building a healthy loan portfolio and achieving an improved risk dispersal. Accordingly, the operational thrust was on achieving a significant reduction in non-performing advances, particularly in the mid-cap segment, which offered chances of a quick recovery. Recognising the vast potential, the management concentrated more on the retail lending segment. The modified schemes for this area evoked an encouraging response, according to the annual report.

Consistent with RBI's guidelines on the risk management system in banks, the management took a number of steps to improve the working of the credit risk management system. For this purpose, a credit risk management committee (CRMC) was constituted. The gaps in the existing risk management practices relating to the credit process were identified and corrective measures taken. The internationally reputed consultancy firm, the Boston Consulting Group, has provided valuable inputs on establishing appropriate risk management systems and the board of directors of PNB has set up an in-house task force to evolve credit risk management tools. A separate credit policy and risk management department has also been set up to undertake the overall implementation of risk management.

CAPITAL ADEQUACY RATIO

PNB's capital to risk asset ratio (CRAR) at 10.31 per cent at the end of March 2000 was higher than the minimum prescription of nine per cent. In order to further augment the capital base, the Bank came out with an initial public offering sometime ago.

NPA MANAGEMENT

During 1999-2000, an added thrust was given to reduction in the level of non-performing assets. A detailed policy on recovery as well as compromise and a negotiated settlement was formulated on the basis of RBI guidelines. Further, a special compromise strategy for the small scale sector under the settlement advisory committee (SAC) was evolved as a one-time measure applicable upto 30th September, 2000. The Bank has introduced pilot projects for recovery of NPAs in the Delhi and Northern Zones of the bank. Recovery task forces have been constituted in these zones and the results are said to be quite encouraging. More such projects have been proposed in other zones of the Bank. Besides, special emphasis has been laid on review/monitoring of accounts with dues of Rs. 1 crore and more. Due to a number of initiatives at different levels and special emphasis on recovery management, the Bank was able to reduce the gross NPAs during the year 1999-2000 (net of addition in existing NPAs) by Rs. 574 crore as compared to Rs. 545 crore in the previous year. The ratio of net NPAs to net advances dropped from 8.96 per cent to 8.52 per cent at the end of March 2000. The recession in industrial segments such as iron and steel, textiles and engineering, a change in the asset classification norms in State Government guaranteed accounts and slippages in loans under Government-sponsored schemes, obviously, contributed to a lower reduction in NPAs.

(D) PROFITING ON BORROWED MONEY

When someone wanted advice from a leading industrialist on a business option for all the wealth he had accumulated, he deservedly got by way of a response a contemptuous look and an angry remark, "you must be a fool to think of using your own money to put in a business. If you really want to be a good businessman, you must use someone else's money". A sensible manager's approach to credit should essentially reflect this time tested entreprenential wisdom. Just as for a finance minister using a rising deficit to meet the nation's varied needs is the elementary rule of sound fiscal management, for the aspiring tycoon getting several people to sustain his ambition is the first step towards corporate czardom. Banks and development financial institutions, the investing public and the Government itself constitute the resource base of an entrepreneur. Banks are tapped to the point where a nexus between industrialists and businessmen develops quickly. Often, this turns unholy and a normal function of business becomes a collusion.

I earlier dealt with various aspects of credit management by the banks. This is only one side of what really is a key aspect of management of banks on the one hand and the running of industry and business sector on the other. There is another side of the coin and this concerns how well or badly the critical act of lending and borrowing is handled. Ideally, there should neither be over lending nor over borrowing. Given the hard fact of banks surviving largely on net interest income, they would not mind over lending where the return is good and where the loan has little prospect of turning sticky. For some years, Hindalco was held up as an example of a corporate entity, which borrowed substantially from banks as well as other sources despite its being a cash rich organisation. Obviously, banks saw in the company's large cash surplus a guarantee of creditworthiness, which we all know, is a core aspect of a bank's credit policy. An economist, who is concerned about efficient resource allocation both at the macro and micro level, will, no doubt, frown on a bank loosening its purse strings to a corporate which is flush with cash. For him, bank loans should, ideally, flow not towards those who do not need support but those who are short of funds.

SCARCITY OF FUNDS

The stipulation of margins and seed capital is intended to inject the requisite discipline in the lender-borrower relationship, but we can see that this also demonstrates the scarcity of capital generally and emphasises the need for prudent management of the resources available. Ideally, not only the banks should exercise the utmost care in the deployment of credit but such descretion should also be willingly practised by those who borrow. Yes, interest payment gives the borrower some tax relief, which otherwise does not come easily. Such relief also reduces the real cost of credit. Obviously, when big industry complains bitterly of rising interest rates and the cost of credit, it conveniently ignores the tax relief that goes with the interest outgo. But, borrowing for the sake of tax saving does not make sense especially in a situation of capital stringency where the need for credit is not particularly urgent. Industry and business can be expected not to resort to needless borrowing since taking on an additional interest burden is commercially indefensible. They are also generally unlikely to overplay a need.

Thus, if and where there is a problem this has to do with

the difference in perception of the need between the lender and borrower. Since banks have to cater to diverse sectors and also have to meet mandatory requirements (priority sector lending, statutory liquidity ratio and cash reserve ratio), they would be tightfisted. Flexibility suffers because of pressure on lendable resources and on credit deployment. Worry over scandals leads to bank officials standing still on requests for additional credit. With the CBI getting increasingly involved in investigations in bank frauds, this may seem quite a natural response. But, industry and business should not be asked to suffer because of this.

NO DILLY-DALLYING

Credit must reach those in urgent need of it and there should be no dilly-dallying. No doubt, the need must be genuine and legitimate. The involvement of the underworld in the financing of the film *chori chori chupke chupke* in some way underlines both the urgency of the need and the fact that legitimate sources of finance were not open to the producer of the film. Obviously, no one would want to tap the criminal gangs knowing all the risks that such tapping carried. It is known that banks do not get into film production unless this is routed through the Film Finance Corporation of India, but as for the soap serials telecast in several TV channels, banks are very much in business. It emerges that in the perception of banks the risks that go with the serials are manageable unlike those of films produced for the big screen. There are, no doubt, exceptions like the evidently faltering programme *Sawal Dus Crore Ka*, which must have caused jitters to the financing banks because of its poor run.

Evidently, this aspect of bank finance pales into insignificance when compared to the level of lending to big industry, the designated priority sectors (which account for 40 per cent of gross bank credit) and business. While it is acknowledged that industry and business do make use of the resources of the parallel economy, black money is not to be confused with what the underworld has to offer. Yes, what all comes through banks is not necessarily white money, going by the bizarre experience of the big U.S. banks turning cocaine-tainted funds into legitimate resources, but then once banks receive a deposit it acquires legitimacy. By the time it gets transformed into a loan its 'whiteness' is further consolidated. White or black, once an advance is made, banks and the borrowers alike — in different, though not contrary, ways obviously — have to make sure that the funds are productively utilised, facilitating the scheduled return of the principal amount and not just the payment of the interest due. NPAs have to be kept minimal and the recovery process must be sound enough to make a healthy level of recycling possible.

NOT THE TRUE COLOURS

The balance sheets of banks as much as those of the big borrowers do not always reveal the true colours. There is a lot of squaring up and adjustments do get made to make the picture as rosy as possible. The various ratios that banks and the debtors have to honour could well undergo a lot of manipulation before these are made acceptable. The phenomenon of NPAs could effectively be more worrying than what is assumed. Indeed, the magnitude of non-performing assets might turn out to be the tip of the proverbial iceberg and nobody might bother about what all the reported figures hide. Rightly, it must be assumed that an acknowledged level of NPAs represents gross ineptness or worse on the part of banks and borrowers alike. A debt service failure reflects much more than what is obvious. True, in any NPA the lending bank's lackadaisical approach to sound utilisation and recovery of what it lent proclaims itself all too loudly. But, this is not all. The performance, more specifically the non-performance, of the borrower is very important and bank monitoring by itself can never be so effective as to ensure that nothing ever goes wrong.

The quarterly information system is allright as far as it

goes but once an advance is made it is not easy to get it back, though as far as the banks' balance sheet is concerned full recovery would be the best thing to do. The long drawn out process of identification of sick enterprises and their revival underscores the difficulty facing banks in pulling a burning finger fast enough to ensure that it is intact. Banks are expected not to operate like Shylock but to go along with the debtors as long as they should — not just can — in their capacity as catalysts. The lender-borrower relationship is not a personal one but involves a healthy sharing of responsibility. Credit management is a great deal more than book keeping, sending out threats and holding legal proceedings. Productive activities in diverse sectors have to be made possible and in this endeavour banks and their borrowers have to collaborate with trust in each other well before a loan is sanctioned and this collaboration must continue until the principal amount is paid back in full. The various ratios and parameters can be expected to fall in line once the basic trust is established.

RECALLING ST. PETER

Credit is essentially a function of giving and taking. But, obviously, it is not so simple as St. Peter had assumed. "Ask, thou shall receive", he had said, but then asking and receiving constitute a complex mechanism. Asking was never an easy proposition and will never be one and giving is also to be treated on the same footing. The relationship between banks and those in need of funds has to be purpose like, professional rather than personal. But, often this deteriorates and acts of fraudulence are a consequence of such a deterioration. The Bible was not simplistic on the matter of asking and receiving. The words of St. Peter hid more than what they had seemed to convey.

The suicide by a senior manager of the Syndicate Bank in Noida in U.P. sometime back in someway underscored the scope for failures in the lender-borrower relationship that was grave enough to make one of the parties take the suicidal route. The ethical aspect of these failures should not be missed lightly. The heroine and the Oscar award winner in the mega film *Titanic* recalls in her ripe old age her fiance 'putting the pistol into his mouth' to put an end to the embarrassment arising out of his business losses during the great depression of 1929. The resort to similar means by the bank official in Noida is another side of the same coin. It is not just that the basic norms of Indian ethics have changed dramatically between 1929 and now, with the lender paying with his life for an act of misplaced trust instead of the debtor, unable to stand the public humiliation of not honouring the trust placed in him by his creditors, taking this extreme step. Even in post-liberalisation India handloom weavers do take their lives year after year demonstrating the extreme moralistic spirit of the debtor in *Titanic.* Values have not changed very much to that extent.

For us what should matter is the fact that there are two to a loan contract and they both should be fully conscious of their contractual obligations. It is not enough for one of the parties to the deal being honourable, obviously not in the mocking sense that Mr. Macawber in *David Copperfield* interpreted this aspect of human conduct while finally exposing his employer, Uriah Heep. One cannot depend on law and the law enforcing authority to promote honourable conduct when the concerned parties themselves fail to take their responsibilities seriously. The policeman is no reformer. True reform must come from within. The inadequacy of loan recovery tribunals was not at the root of the growth of NPAs. The malady was much deeper. The commitment to the viability of a loan must be inherent, not superficial. It must be self-driven, not created under duress. In this context, the role of CBI and CVC must be supportive, not displacing.

ANSWERABILITY OF BORROWERS

One aspect of credit management that has failed to receive requisite attention is the answerability of managers at different levels for defaults in repayment of loans and payment of interest. When those who sanction advances either punish themselves or are punished by managements — with or without vigilance agencies playing a part — it becomes incumbent on regulators or those who sit in judgement over growth of NPAs to take an increasingly objective view of managerial responsibility in the banking sector specifically and the financial sector generally. Over time, several loan sanctioning officials have had to face disciplinary proceedings because of the loans becoming sticky. Granted that the trust they placed in certain borrowers had proved to be misplaced, still there could not have been any criminal intent in the choice of debtors and the decision to provide the financial support sought. It is known that advances do often get sanctioned because of pressure from above. That documentary evidence was not always available to the managers concerned to prove their innocence rendered it all the more necessary to have safety mechanisms in place for managers caught in an embarrassing position later on.

Investigating and audit agencies may not bother too much about such mechanisms, but those really concerned about making banking activity more and more professional certainly have to address seriously this aspect. Obviously, loans, big or small, have to be sanctioned by committees, rather than by individual managers. More importantly, members of the committees also should not be blamed and asked to face the consequences of borrowers failing to honour their side of the bargain. Committees, obviously, are less likely to be pushed or pulled by superior officers and extraneous forces than individual managers. Even if they are hustled they can be expected to safeguard their interests by noting somewhere that they acted only at the behest of this or that person. While this option is not always closed to individuals, such noting by the latter may fail to receive serious notice and to the advantage of the officials in the dock because nobody will be prepared to endorse these notings. One must remember in this context that a middle level official working for a constitutional functionary currently is having problems not only proving his own bonafides but also establishing the responsibility of a higher authority for a decision, which in his own assessment went against the neutral character of the functionary.

FIXING OFFICIALS

Fraudulence and an unholy collusion with the borrowers have to be established firmly before an official is fixed. Mere suspicion should not do to provoke disciplinary action. It is wrong to suspect the worst from any NPA and loan sanctioning should be encouraged to grow into a purely professional practice. What the CBI understands as criminal intent should not be interpreted indiscriminately in regard to banking activity and the Vigilance Commission should stop taking an unduly moralistic view of defaults in loan recovery. If productive activities in various segments of the economy have to be fostered, bank officials should be encouraged to trust those coming to them with requests for financial assistance. A regime must be promoted where managers at various levels do not any longer have to fear the worst from honest mistakes. This alone can give banking a totally professional character, free from political or other pressures.

III

EMERGING MARKETS IN THE NEW FINANCIAL SYSTEM: MANAGING FINANCIAL AND CORPORATE DISTRESS

There was an IMF/World Bank seminar in March-April, 2000, which focussed on the very issues that should concern Indian policymakers and, even more so, bank officials at different levels. Here in a nutshell are the different stages of a crisis situation and the appropriate corrective mechanism based on the discussions at the seminar.

Coverage

- Pre-crisis
  - ❑ Predictors / early warning indicators
  - ❑ Underlying reasons
  - Crisis prevention
- Crisis handling
  - ❑ Corporate and bank restructuring

Predictors

- The key indicator is short term debt (STD) / capital flow

- Short term debt consists of
  - ❑ Trade credit
  - ❑ Portfolio flows (debt instruments only, equity flows generally not included)
  - ❑ Private and public commercial paper
  - ❑ Inter-bank deposits

Indicators

- Short term debt / M2 (money stock)> 1
- Forex reserves / short term debt < 1
- Forex reserves covering less than 4 months' payments of all kinds, trade as well as non-trade.
- A high Government and financial sector component in STD increases risk
- A higher trade credit component in STD decreases risk

Early Warning System

- Fundamentals
- Current A/c Deficit
- Export growth
- Real exchange rate depreciation
- Short term Indicators
- Forex reserves
- Short term Debt / M2

Reasons

- Push and pull factors

- Structural, cyclical and policy factors

Parity Framework

Pull Factors - I

- Structural
- Deregulation (corporate borrowing)
- Cyclical
- High interest rates in emerging financial markets + low interest rates in developed markets Tendency of local firms to borrow abroad

Pull Factors - (II)

- Policy
- Tax and other incentives for short term debt
  - ❑ Deregulation of domestic banks
  - ❑ Interest rate parity actively held in abeyance through bank activity

Push Factors

- Structural
  - ❑ New technologies (telecom.etc.) — low transactions costs
- Cyclical
  - ❑ Low rates of interest in industrialised countries
- Policy
  - ❑ Existing BIS (Bank of International Settlements) capital adequacy ratio formula

Reaction

- The response of short term debt to cyclical shocks
  - ❑ Pro-cyclical
  - ❑ More on the downside; exaggerates adverse shocks

Derivatives - (I)

- Off-balance sheet products make balance sheet / BoP information incomplete / unreliable
- Increased ability to separate and market risks across countries and markets
  - ❑ long and short term; different currencies; debt and equity; floating and fixed interest rates)

Derivatives - (II)

- Derivatives can be used to avoid prudential regulations and take highly leveraged positions

Reasons for a crisis

- An excessively close relationship between Government and companies.
- Monopoly and favouritism; poor corporate governance
- Dependence on Government support and policy protection
- Low levels of efficiency; uncompetitive without protection; stiff restrictions on foreign competition
- Conglomerates with political connections — horizontal and vertical integration — non-core activities; a jungle of cross subsidies
- Excessive lending by banks

- Dollar debt dependent + highly leveraged

Slow pace of corporate restructuring

- Failure to recognise problems
- Overvaluation of assets vs. market
- Inadequate incentives to restructure
- Macro-economic recovery could undermine corporate restructuring, when there is no significant change in fundamentals

Self-Protection Policies

- Exchange rate flexibility
  - ❑ Letting interest rate parity prevail
- Forex reserves accumulation
- Signing up contingent credit lines
- Capital controls
  - ❑ To match the better maturity of domestic assets and foreign liabilities
  - ❑ Tobin Tax - a proportionate tax on capital inflow / outflow
  - ❑ Imposing an one time tax on inflows
  - ❑ Contingent controls on cash outflows — restrictions
  - ❑ Direct controls on short term bank borrowing

Risk Handling

- For corporates as well as countries
  - ❑ Risk assessment
  - ❑ Risk management

Risk Assessment

- Knowing the current economic condition (on a market-to-market basis)
- Measuring quantifiable risk
  - ❑ Market risk; Credit risk; Liquidity risk
- Qualitatively monitor a less quantifiable risk
  - ❑ Operational / business risk

Risk Management

- Hedging risk
- Diversifing or insuring unhedged risk
- Manage the capital structure in the light of risk
- Ensuring total transparency / communication about the financial conditions and risks

Crisis Handling: Government Objectives

- Developing a sound banking system (bank restructuring)
- Restoring the creditworthiness of firms (corporate restructuring)
- Promoting economic growth
- Minimising cost to the Government

Corporate Restructuring: The ideal practices

- Ensuring the prompt ability of creditors to appoint receivers, seize and sell collateral
- Having a court-supervised re-organisation framework
  - ❑ giving an opportunity for work-outs
  - ❑ deadlines

  - ❑ majority creditor approval

- Having agreed standards among financial institutions for work-outs
- Prompting substantial institutional capacity
- Having strong regulators
- Ensuring that there are no legal and tax barriers for restructuring
- Providing adequate public resources for bank recapitalisation + systematic monitoring
- To have AMCs operating totally on the basis of commercial principles

Corporate debt restructuring options

- Roll-overs
- Reduced interest rates
- Debt write-downs
- Assets in lieu of debt
- Debt-equity swaps

Factors influencing corporate restructuring

- Speed of macro-economic recovery
- The political environment
- Institutional capacity
- Magnitude of corporate debt
- Ability to impose losses on debtors
- Willingness and ability of creditors to recognise losses

Government's role

- Crisis prevention

- Restricting access to risky capital
- Monitoring unsustainable over-investment by corporates

- Crisis response
  - Re-organisation, liquidation and creditor protection
  - Corporate restructuring
  - Having an enabling environment
- Honest broker / mediator
- Adopting a more active variant of the London approach (detailed below)
- Establishing a sound framework
- Ensuring a proper linkage between bank recapitalisation and corporate debt restructuring

London Approach

- Evolved by the Bank of England in the seventies
- The direct role of the Government and central bank getting gradually reduced to that of a catalyst or diplomat
- Creditors initially consider non-statutory measures
- Creditors commission an independent review of long term viability
- An informal standstill by banks during the period of review
- After review, creditors take a joint view
  - Steering Committee + Lead Bank
- After discussions and an agreement a more lasting form of financial support is provided for

The East Asian Approach

- This involves a more direct role for central bank / Government
- Ad hoc institutions for corporate work-outs are created with extensive powers
- Creating incentives and eliminating impediments through laws and guidelines + effective judicial system
- Giving an integrated corporate — in addition to a financial sector — focus

Framework Establishment

- Establishing a suitable tax and legal environment
- Formulating an effective debt restructuring framework
- Separation of viable from non-viable corporations
- Financial engineering — Debt reduction, D/E swaps etc.

Environment

- Legal framework
  - ❑ An insolvency and out-of-court settlement regime
  - ❑ Legal limits on foreign ownership
- Tax Issues
  - ❑ Capital gains during restructuring
  - ❑ Temporary tax relief deductions/ deductions / subsidies

Crisis Resolution

- Government to monitor the health of major corporate

sectors

- Segmenting the crisis and prioritising the various possible responses
- Exit for non-viable companies
- Formal out-of-court processes to deal with bankruptcies / NPAs and inter-creditor disputes, backed up by court-supervised seizure, foreclosure and liquidation
- Willingness to restructure and take on losses without threatening current shareholders indiscriminately.
- Tax breaks
- Debt restructuring
    - ❑ Finding out where the money went when the crisis happened
    - ❑ Establishment of credit rating agencies

The Government's Role in Facilitating Bank Restructuring

- Institutional and legal framework for restructuring
- Criteria for evaluating institutions
- A differential strategy for non-viable and viable institutions
- Defining the modalities of public sector support for restructuring
- Arrangements for loan recovery and work-outs and AMCs;
- Operational restructuring
- Compliance with prudential norms and provisioning

The Approach to Viable Institutions

- Recapitalisation by existing shareholders besides proportionate / matching contributions from the Government
- Government contributions as debt/equity/guarantees
- Nationalisation / temporary take-over by the Government
- Foreign capital limits raised
- Purchase of NPAs
- Existing shareholders to bear losses till the capital is written off
- Closures, mergers, purchase and assumption operations and bridge banks

Bank Restructuring

- Contractual agreements between
    - Governments and banks (or principal shareholders, if not diluted)
    - Banks and senior managers

Corporate Debt Restructuring by Banks

- A trilateral approach preferred to a bilateral approach
    - Government involvement as a principal
- Methods
    - Case-by-case approach (centralised / decentralised)
    - Pool / portfolio method

Government Costs in Restructuring

- Paying out guaranteed liabilities and providing liquidity support
- Assistance in meeting CARs
- Purchase of NPAs
- 15-45 per cent of GDP = gross costs

Controllable Sources of Costs

- Carrying costs for assets on which debt service is suspended
- Bail out of debtors
- Looting — by shareholders, managers or employees of banks/companies
    - ❑ due to uncertainty / lack of controls
- Waste — Government support not put to effective use
    - ❑ without necessary restructuring

Collective Action for Restructuring Sovereign Debt

- Collective action clauses not mandatory in US issues of sovereign bonds (unlike those of the U. K.)
- The moral hazard of overlending
    - ❑ IMF augmented resources as a safety net
    - ❑ No forgiveness or interruption in interest payments; only rescheduling
- Need for burden sharing by "bailing in" private sector creditors
- Recognising that it is impossible to distinguish reliably between illiquidity and insolvency for sovereign debt and proceeding on this basis

- ❑ IMF lending may fuel panic, precipitating creditor exit and creating an unacceptable moral hazard

- Collective action clauses to permit debt restructuring (on a corporate pattern)
  - ❑ This would, no doubt, raise the cost of borrowing, but not lead to an inability to borrow
  - ❑ Avoid a moral hazard
  - ❑ The creation of a bondholders committee would facilitate *post facto* restructuring

Financial Stability Forum (FSF)

- Set up in April 1999, this is designed to promote international financial stability through information exchange and international co-operation in financial supervision and surveillance

FSF Membership

- G7 countries
- Institutional members
- Other members
- Countries, which are members of working groups

FSF Activities

- Working groups for
  - ❑ Highly leveraged Institutions (HLIs);
  - ❑ Capital flows;
  - ❑ Offshore financial centres
- A compendium of international standards for financial systems

Country Case — Thailand

- Debt-financed expansion into highly competitive sectors outside core competencies
- Weak regulations in the corporate and financial sectors
- Poor disclosure / transparency
- Weak corporate governance
- A high degree of related party transactions / cronyism

Thailand - Lessons

- Corporate restructuring
  - ❑ Out-of-court settlements
  - ❑ Time-bound
  - ❑ Avoiding a "moral hazard"
- Non-Performing Loans / Assets
  - ❑ Transfer to asset management companies backed by the Government
  - ❑ Concentration and securitisation

South Korean Crisis

- Reasons
  - ❑ High leveraging
  - ❑ Conglomerate investment in diverse sectors
  - ❑ Neglect of standard financial performance parameters

South Korean Restructuring

- Financial sector restructuring related to corporate restructuring

- Best corporate restructuring regime
  - The financial supervisory commission
  - A sound insolvency regime
  - A capital structure improvement programme for the top five *chaebols*
- For *chaebols* ranked from 6 to 64 a good corporate work-out programme
  - A sound corporate restructuring accord
  - A steering committee and a corporate restructuring coordination committee of creditors
- A programme for small and medium enterprises
- Setting up a South Korean AMC

IV

ISSUES IN PERSPECTIVE

These are the objective perceptions of an expert based overseas who wishes to remain anonymous because of his professional commitments. What appears here is a well-considered response to certain queries put to him.

Job insecurity is probably too strong a phrase. What you have in mind is job security irrespective of performance. The US style of complete job insecurity, where jobs are created and lost instantaneously (based on fractional percentage point changes in economic indicators, among other factors), has a social cost, which cannot be underestimated and will probably be impossible to implement in a country like India without any social security safety net. However, the fact remains that recruitment, remuneration and termination must be made much more flexible than at present. Also, a monolithic style of negotiation between the IBA and staff associations ignores the fact that different banks are performing differently, and the staff therein must be treated differently. Industry-wide negotiations will not help in differentiating between well-run and badly run banks.

BANK RESTRUCTURING

I am referring to the series of papers presented at the IMF/World Bank seminar. Some of the ideas are worth incorporating in the study. The main idea is that bank restructuring should, ideally, be taken together with corporate restructuring. Except for South Korea, in all other countries, corporate restructuring has lagged behind bank/ FI restructuring. Governments have focussed on recapitalising banks in various ways, without tackling the underlying corporate restructuring, which is more urgently required. NPAs have arisen primarily because of corporate failures. Hence, the recommendation of tying Government support for bank recapitalisation with prompt and aggressive action on work-outs for corporate failures to repay.

The trick is in balancing the "moral hazard" (i.e. the tendency of bank debtors to get off too lightly) against a highly creditor-oriented situation (typical of Government-owned organisations), where any write-off / settlement requires excessively high levels of authority, approvals, explanations and fixing/ assignment of responsibility, resulting in a scenario where it is organisationally more favourable to bury a problem rather than to solve it. The problem is that bad debts should be treated like a batting average — have a cut off percentage in terms of bad debts for the portfolio for each division (a carefully set percentage should neither be too low, leading to an extreme risk aversion, nor too high, which could lead to excessively risky lending). Unfortunately, Governmental organisations' rules and regulations (compounded by CVC/ CBI investigations) are not designed for averages; these focus on individual cases (which creates a phobia for not taking decisions at all — you will never be wrong, if you don't decide).

The apparent success story of South Korea in work-outs is probably attributable to political will (a new President with no political baggage) and an excellent structural framework for the *chaebol* improvement programme with extremely tough deadlines for work-outs, failing which there will be a binding arbitration, with insolvency as a back-up option.

While I do not know the full details of the Indian action programme for handling NPAs, the brief given in your introduction does not look encouraging enough. Settlement advisory committees are just not enough; such committees will recommend and nothing more. We need binding recommendations, with disagreements to be handled within a stipulated time frame by arbitration. Of course, we should have a cut-off period as well as a discriminating attitude towards different borrowers to avoid the "moral hazard" and also not to penalise genuine borrowers unduly. One advantage that India should have, unlike other countries, is that banks (being mainly Government- owned) are more likely to agree together on collective work-outs; the problem of minority creditors preventing work-outs is less likely here (this has been tackled in countries like South Korea, by ensuring that only 75 per cent of the creditors need to approve the work-out).

Generally, in most of the crisis-ridden countries, AMCs for purchasing NPAs have not been considered very successful. These have generally been seen as an incentive to "moral hazard", in a sense rewarding banks for bad lending. At the same time, Governments have been less than keen to either fund AMCs fully or properly (ensuring that instead of sick banks, you have sick AMCs), or take aggressive action through the AMCs against the creditors. The only real advantage of AMCs is the concentration of creditors against a single borrower, facilitating better collective action. As I have stated earlier, I don't think that collective action is really a major problem with Indian banks — the problem is the action itself. In the Indian scenario, there is one other advantage — if the Government is clear that it will impose a tough, competitive regime for public sector banks to operate in, it may be worthwhile considering AMCs to buy off past NPAs to give them a clean slate to start from, with no competitive disadvantages.

Regarding financial restructuring, in addition to operational and organisational restructuring, there is also a need to link re-capitalisation with the progress of collective work-outs. One other issue that the crisis countries have faced is that attaining the CAR norms and adequate doubtful debt provisioning are almost mutually incompatible in the initial stages of bank restructuring. If you provision adequately, it becomes more difficult to achieve the required CAR. Therefore, initially, Governments have laid more emphasis on CAR, gradually tightening the provisioning norms year by year.

Regarding the financial restructuring agency, the recommended practice is to have a single agency with full responsibility and authority. Countries like Indonesia and Thailand, where multiple agencies — the Ministry of Finance, the central bank and the restructuring agency — have had the requisite authority, have fared worse than South Korea, where there is a single supervening agency – the Financial Restructuring Council.

BANK COMPUTERISATION

While banks, for instance, in Oman are probably financially and operationally much weaker than their Indian counterparts, one area of major success is computerisation. All banks have complete computerisation of all accounts (even the local Bank of Baroda has full internal computerisation of all banking transactions). In addition, they (but not the Bank of Baroda) have a wide range of automated teller machines (ATMs) and point of shopping (POS) terminals besides the facility of online telephone banking and electronic payment of water, electricity as well as telephone bills. This ensures that (a) customers have full on-line (24 hours) access to banking anywhere and any time and (b) transaction costs are lower because of no manual intervention. In India, banks like the Citibank have been very aggressive with ATMs, especially in places like Bangalore. However, public sector banks like SBI do not need to do so much. It has been estimated that for servicing the majority of its corporate clients (its bread and butter), SBI would need to just provide on-line linked computer access at about 30-40 locations throughout the country. Public sector banks would do well to start with areas and places, where the maximum returns are likely to be received. (This is exactly the approach followed by the Indian Railways in expanding its computerised reservation system - start with very high volume stations, move in a phased manner to other stations and leave a large number of very small stations still manually operated (without computerised reservation), where it is just not cost-effective.

Regarding the software available for banks, I don't agree fully with what you say in the introduction. I'm sure, there are lots of small outfits, but I know that companies like Infosys are camping in countries like Oman to sell their Indian developed banking software to banks against stiff competition from Western developed software. The problem, I suspect, is that banks (like most Indian organisations — public and, to some extent, private) do not really put the right price tag on computer software.

DERIVATIVES

With the legacy of exchange controls, most banks in India (public and private sector and foreign) would not have played the derivatives game. With the increasing sophistication of the free market and with more market players in the game (and the free entry that will have to be allowed to foreign banks within a few years in line with WTO regulations), derivatives (off-balance sheet products) are likely to be used to separate market risks across countries as well as across markets. Traditional exchange / capital controls as well as the IMS Balance of Payment information tend to be inadequate. E.g.

- traditionally, long term foreign debt is supposed to be less risky than short term debt. On paper, corporates / banks may issue long term debt abroad and then swap it into short term commercial paper.
- Equity is supposedly less fluid than debt. Corporates could issue equity and then swap it against debt.

This requires extensive transparency and disclosure norms, as well as continuous monitoring by the RBI to evaluate the impact of such products on the traditional BoP information.

AUTHOR'S COMMENTS

The views expressed by the expert are difficult to brush aside. But, I must reaffirm my want of confidence in the bureaucracy of Indian banks, particularly those supposedly under public control, in pushing their entities on the reforming path. The expert writes of on-line computer access, but he should know that bank officials here do not even take the trouble of finding out — that too for as long as seven months and even more — whether or not the banks' software suppliers are alive or dead. One swallow does not make a summer, goes the saying, but I suppose that one example based on my personal experience is enough to show up the ineptness of supervisory staff in banks as much as the lack of professionalism of software companies. On April 24, 2000, I got a telephone connection, which I learnt soon after had been used earlier by a software company, Numeric Power Systems. Then my woes begun and these do not seem like ending.

Not a day passes without bank staff — this may be of the PNB, Indian Bank, Indian Overseas Bank, UCO Bank or the Central Bank of India — repeatedly harassing me, and my explanation that this is my home and not the office of Numeric goes in vain. I do not doubt that some of the best known names in the Indian infotech sector are determined to establish a strong presence in the overseas market, but I also know of outfits like Numeric not bothering to tell their customers that their telephone numbers have changed. Even if some of these companies close down, courtesy demands that they should keep their erstwhile customers informed. While I do mind the harassment, what worries me more is the lethargy — that is contrary to the essential spirit of liberalisation and reform — explicit in the obviously mechanical assumption by bank officials that their software suppliers operate from either my drawing room or bedroom and the refusal to believe the hard fact that when they call up my residential number the phone rings in my drawing room, and not the office of Numeric.

On debt restructuring, an area covered by the IMF/World Bank seminar, some progress has been achieved with various banks and FIs agreeing to form a corporate debt restructuring cell for shortening the time taken for decisions on defaulter accounts. The cell would be concerned with accounts of over Rs. 20 crore. The cell would decide on whether to opt for restructuring the debt or go in for legal action against defaulters within a time frame of 180 days. Under the cell, there will be committees on separate defaulting companies constituted by representatives of banks and FIs that are part of the funding consortia. Decisions will be taken on the basis of a majority of 60 or 75 per cent.

Now, all this is very good on paper. But, this arrangement has to work and very fast, and effectively, if a dent has to be made on NPAs, that add up to a massive Rs. 60,000 crore, of which provisioning has been done only for Rs. 25,000 crore. Significantly, 0.5 per cent of the defaulters account for 60 per cent of the total NPAs.

V

SOFTWARE: A HAZARDOUS AREA

By R. Y. Seshan
Banking Software Expert

During the initial stages of computerisation, the nationalised banks instead of taking the traditional hardware and software system chose a small PC-based software as the means of computerisation. The PC-based software comprises a small system catering only to the front office on a customer- related module. This created a revolution of sorts in that the banking industry could be controlled by a small-PC based framework. The package used in the PC is called ALPM (automatic ledger posting machine). The Reserve Bank of India contributed to the next phase known as total branch automation (TBA), through a networking of PCs or the dummy terminal connected to each other and to the database centrally located in the branch itself. The total branch automation package not only caters to the front office system but also the back office system of branches. Under ALPM, computers are not connected to each other and customers have to go to a particular counter for transactions, but with the TBA module of computerisation the customer is free to operate from any mode or terminal and transact in the account. This phase has given the customer value-added services like passbook printing, lobby banking, remote banking and tele banking. So far, since the nationalised banks spread throughout the country did not have a proper, reliable and cheap mode of communication network as in the developed countries they were dependent on total branch automation. But, with the opening up of the telecommunication sector multiple branch and cluster banking is going to be the order of the day.

PRIVATE Vs NATIONALISED BANKS

In contrast to their public sector counterparts, the private banks have access to the latest and fastest technology and are fast eating into the customer base and capturing particularly the cream pie customers of nationalised banks. The latter are still stuck with the old procedure of opening a branch and then hunting for customers, but the technology-rich private banks identify the prospective customers first and start the branches in appropriate locations. They then lure more customers. Customers are attracted to the tech-savvy private banks because of their being able to access their accounts from any nook and corner of the country. By accessing the ATM, they can withdraw or deposit funds from wherever they want to. Public sector banks are facing an acute shortage of computer-trained staff since private banks and software companies alike are taking away such personnel. The banking software industry is now up for grabs, with the global majors slowly shifting their bases to India. This segment is not controlled under any law or guidelines from statutory bodies even after 20 years of computerisation and no standard reports are required by statutory auditors and, what is more, the internal audit requirement of reports also varies from banks to banks and branches to branches.

We face a somewhat complex situation because the software that claims to be of the total branch automation variety still follows the ALPM or PC-based banking solution, which is not fully shareable and is also technologically very backward. A decade ago, when the number one nationalised bank decided to tender globally for software, none of the

Indian software firms was in the list of bidders. Also, the few international banking software companies which participated in the bids could only boast of a technology that was 25 years old. As for banks, they went for such technology precisely because they knew that it was time tested. Many of the Indian banking software companies do not have proper documentation and a sound user or system manual despite running the branches for more than a decade. Also, very few of the firms have an effective quality control inspection of the software after it is developed. Most software is directly ported or developed in the customer site itself. Because of the low cost, banks presently opt for Indian software firms, but the latter don't plan the software design first before coding the package. In fact, they start developing the package in a short span of time with an improper design and the file/data base structure is also not finalised. Sometimes, the software is ported and implemented in bank branches with just 25 per cent of the whole package in readiness and the balance 75 per cent is developed in the customer site. It is high time that the governing bodies of banks took appropriate action and introduced a code for the software requirements of the banks. It must be recognised that with inter-connectivity, there is considerable scope for manipulation. Even a programmer who has left a software company two or three years earlier can visit any of the branches and give the password and access the machine.

WANTED: A FOOLPROOF REMEDY

Banking software is of two types. One is the voucher-based system and the other is the module-based system. The branches that report most problems are those which use the module-based software. Each and every part in the module is related in someway to the reports generated, but the module-based system remains the same. The governing bodies should take a serious note of all these problems and provide a fool proof remedy. Often, software is selected not because it satisfies all the requirements as it should but is simply thrust on banks because of other reasons. The software shown during the demonstration by the firm is not always the same as supplied. Branches do not have any say and often, the head office forces on them untested packages. As a remedy to this, a nationalised bank sometime ago started a software subsidiary in collaboration with other banks. But, the exercise failed since none of the promoting banks gave orders to the subsidiary.

Generally, banking software firms are flourishing because of RBI insisting on computerisaton of at least 70 per cent of banking business in the country. The RBI or any other regulatory body for banking software should develop a mode of interlinking of branches. It should also study all the existing banking packages and evolve a proper code as well as methodology. There are many loopholes in banking software and anyone can access data in the branches. If the data are stored in an open-ended mechanism like internet, there can be serious complications in the banking industry without a proper safety mechanism. An untrained banking software operator, for his part, can cause a mini-crisis. With the emergence of any bank branch (ABB) banking or cluster banking in the second phase of computerisation, effective checks have become urgent and regulators should facilitate digital storing of old data in lieu of the traditional hard copy of printed data. The packages should have data mining and housing capability should be built into packages. The present packages do not in any way use the full functionality of the operating system. It is necessary to incorporate many of the accounting, auditing and user maintenance data from the operating system. Bank branches do not follow a standard method of storage and data management. The regulators should recheck the whole design and patent it and seal the main core packages developed by the software companies and only leave some parts of the system for banks to customise their area of application.

[*The views expressed in the presentation strictly represent the personal opinions of the expert.*]

VI

BIS CRITERIA FOR EFFECTIVE BANKING SUPERVISION

The Basel Committee on Banking Supervision of the Bank of International Settlements (BIS) has formulated a number of core principles for effective banking supervision. These add up to 25 and are critical to sound management of banking activity in the country especially under a process of liberalisation. Promoting a clear understanding of the principles and the respective criteria should be an important goal of any meaningful strategy.

Principle 1: An effective system of banking supervision will have clear responsibilities and objectives for each agency involved in the supervision of banks. Each such agency should possess operational independence and adequate resources. A suitable legal framework for banking supervision is also necessary, including provisions relating to authorisation of banking establishments and their ongoing supervision; powers to address compliance with laws as well as safety and soundness concerns; and legal protection for supervisors. Arrangements for sharing information between supervisors and protecting the confidentiality of such information should be in place.

Note: Principle 1 is divided into six component parts. Four of the component parts are not repeated elsewhere in the core principles. However, two parts (3 & 4) are developed in greater detail in one or more of the subsequent principles. For these two, since the criteria will be developed further elsewhere, this section identifies only the most fundamental and crucial ones.

1(1): An effective system of banking supervision will have clear responsibilities and objectives for each agency involved in the supervision of banks.

Essential criteria

1. Laws are in place for banking, and for (each of) the agency (agencies) involved in banking supervision. The responsibilities and objectives of each of the agencies are clearly defined.
2. The laws and/or supporting regulations provide a framework of minimum prudential standards that banks must meet.
3. There is a defined mechanism for coordinating actions between agencies responsible for banking supervision and evidence that it is used in practice.
4. The supervisor participates in deciding when and how to effect the orderly resolution of a problem bank situation (which could include closure and assisting in restructuring or merger with a stronger institution).
5. Banking laws are updated as necessary to ensure that these remain effective and relevant to changing industry as well as regulatory practices.

Additional criteria

1. The supervisory agency sets out objectives and is subject to a regular review of its performance set against its responsibilities and objectives through a transparent reporting and assessment process.
2. The supervisory agency ensures that information on

the financial strength and performance of the industry under its jurisdiction is publicly available.

1(2): Each such agency should possess operational independence as well as adequate resources.

Essential criteria

1. There is, in practice, no significant evidence of Government or industry interference in the operational independence of each agency and in each agency's ability to obtain and deploy the resources needed to carry out its mandate.
2. The supervisory agency and its staff have credibility based on their professionalism and integrity.
3. Each agency is financed in a manner that does not undermine its autonomy or independence and permits it to conduct effective supervision and oversight. This includes, *inter alia*:
   - salary scales that allow it to attract and retain qualified staff;
   - the ability to hire outside experts to deal with special situations;
   - a training budget and programme that provides regular training opportunities for staff;
   - a budget for computers and other equipment sufficient to equip its staff with tools needed to review the banking industry; and
   - a travel budget that allows appropriate on-site work.

Additional criteria

1. The head of each agency is appointed for a minimum

term and can be removed from office during such term only for reasons specified in law.

2. Where the head of an agency is removed from office, the reasons must be publicly disclosed.

1(3): A suitable legal framework for banking supervision is also necessary, including provisions relating to authorisation of banking establishments and their ongoing supervision.

Note: This component of principle 1 is amplified considerably in the principles dealing with *Licensing and Structure* (2 to 5), *Prudential Regulation and Requirements* (6 to 15), *Methods of Ongoing Banking Supervision* (16 - 20) and *Information Requirements* (21).

Essential criteria

1. The law identifies the authority (or authorities) responsible for granting and withdrawing banking licences.
2. The law empowers the supervisor to set prudential rules administratively (without changing laws).
3. The law empowers the supervisor to require information from the banks in the form and frequency it deems necessary.

1(4): A suitable legal framework for banking supervision is also necessary, including powers to address compliance with laws as well as safety and soundness concerns.

Note: This component of principle 1 is amplified in principle 22, which addresses the formal powers of supervisors.

Essential criteria

1. The law enables the supervisor to address compliance

with laws and the safety and soundness of the banks under its supervision.

2. The law permits the supervisor to apply qualitative judgement in forming this opinion.

3. The supervisor has unfettered access to banks' files in order to review compliance with internal rules and limits as well as external laws and regulations.

4. When, in a supervisor's judgement, a bank is not complying with laws and regulations or it is or is likely to be engaged in unsafe or unsound practices, the law empowers the supervisor to:

   - take (and/or require a bank to take) prompt remedial action;
   - impose a range of sanctions (including the revocation of the banking licence).

1(5): A suitable legal framework for banking supervision is also necessary, including legal protection for supervisors.

Essential criteria

1. The law provides legal protection to the supervisory agency and its staff against lawsuits for actions taken while discharging their duties in good faith.
2. The supervisory agency and its staff are adequately protected against the costs of defending their actions while discharging their duties.

1(6): Arrangements for sharing information between supervisors and protecting the confidentiality of such information should be in place.

Essential criteria

1. There is a system of cooperation and information

sharing between all domestic agencies with responsibility for the soundness of the financial system.

2. There is a system of cooperation and information sharing with foreign agencies that have supervisory responsibilities for banking operations of material interest to the domestic supervisor.

3. The supervisor

   - may provide confidential information to another financial sector supervisor;
   - is required to take reasonable steps to ensure that any confidential information released to another supervisor will be treated as such by the receiving party;
   - is required to take reasonable steps to ensure that any confidential information released to another supervisor will be used only for supervisory purposes.

4. The supervisor is able to deny any demand (other than a court order or mandate from a legislative body) for confidential information in its possession.

Principle 2: The permissible activities of institutions that are licensed and subject to supervision as banks must be clearly defined and the use of the word "bank" in names should be controlled as far as possible.

Essential criteria

1. The term "bank" is clearly defined in law or regulations.

2. The permissible activities of institutions that are licensed and subject to supervision as banks are clearly defined either by supervisors or in laws or

regulations.

3. The use of the word "bank" and any derivations such as "banking" in a name are limited to the licensed and supervised institutions in all circumstances where the general public otherwise might be misled.

4. The taking of proper bank deposits[2] from the public is reserved for institutions that are licensed and subject to supervision.

Principle 3: The licensing authority must have the right to set criteria and reject applications for establishments that do not meet the standards set. The licensing process, at the minimum, should consist of an assessment of the banking organisation's ownership structure, directors and senior management, its operating plan and internal controls and its projected financial condition, including its capital base; where the proposed owner or parent organisation is a foreign bank, the prior consent of its home country supervisor should be obtained.

Essential criteria

1. The licensing authority has the right to set the criteria for licensing banks. These may be based on the criteria set in law or regulation.

2. The criteria for issuing licences are consistent with those applied in ongoing supervision.

3. The licensing authority has the right to reject applications if the criteria are not fulfilled or if the information provided is inadequate.

4. The licensing authority determines that the proposed legal and managerial structures of the bank will not hinder effective supervision.

[2] An example of a "proper" bank deposit is one that is not subject to security law disclosure requirements.

5. The licensing authority determines the suitability of major shareholders, transparency of ownership structure and the source of initial capital.

6. A minimum initial capital amount is stipulated for all banks.

7. The licensing authority evaluates the proposed directors and senior management as to their expertise and integrity. The criteria include: (1) skills and experience in relevant financial operations commensurate with the intended activities of the bank and (2) no record of criminal activities or adverse regulatory judgements that make a person unfit to uphold important positions in a bank.

8. The licensing authority reviews the proposed strategic and operating plans of the bank. This includes determining that an appropriate system of corporate governance will be in place.

9. The operational structure is required to include, *inter alia*, adequate operational policies and procedures, internal control procedures and an appropriate monitoring of the bank's various activities. The operational structure is required to reflect the scope and degree of sophistication of the proposed activities of the bank.

10. The licensing authority reviews *pro forma* financial statements and projections for the proposed bank. This includes an assessment of the adequacy of the financial strength to support the proposed strategic plan as well as financial information on the principal shareholders of the bank.

11. If the licensing authority and the supervisory authority are not the same, the supervisor has the legal right to have its views considered on each specific application.

12. In the case of foreign banks establishing a branch or subsidiary, prior consent (or at least a statement of "no objection") of the home country supervisor is obtained.

13. If the licensing or supervisory authority determines that the licence was knowingly based on false information, the licence can be revoked.

Additional criteria

1. The assessment of the application includes the ability of shareholders to supply additional financial support, if needed.

2. At least one of the directors must have a sound knowledge of each type of financial activities the bank intends to pursue.

3. The licensing authority has procedures in place to monitor the progress of new entrants in meeting their business and strategic goals and to determine that the supervisory requirements outlined in the licence approval are being met.

Principle 4: Banking supervisors must have the authority to review and reject any proposal to transfer significant ownership or controlling interests in existing banks to other parties.

Essential criteria

1. Law or regulation contains a clear definition of "significant" ownership.

2. There are requirements to obtain supervisory approval[3] or provide immediate notification of proposed changes that would result in a change in

[3] Supervisory approval may consist of either explicit prior approval or non-objection to a prior notification.

ownership or the exercise of voting rights over a particular threshold or change in the controlling interest.

3. The supervisor has the authority to reject any proposal for a change in significant ownership or controlling interest or prevent the exercise of voting rights in respect of such investments, if they do not meet the criteria comparable to those used for approving new banks.

Additional criteria

1. Supervisors obtain from banks, either through periodic reporting or on-site examination, the names and holdings of all significant shareholders, including, if possible, the identities of beneficial owners of shares being held by the custodians.

Principle 5: Banking supervisors must have the authority to establish criteria for reviewing major acquisitions or investments by a bank and ensuring that corporate affiliations or structures do not expose it to undue risks or hinder effective supervision.

Essential criteria

1. Laws or regulations clearly define what types and amounts (absolute and/or in relation to a bank's capital) of acquisitions and investments need supervisory approval[4].

2. Laws or regulations provide criteria by which to judge individual proposals.

3. Consistent with the licensing requirements, among the objective criteria that the supervisor uses is that any new acquisitions and investments do not expose

---

[4] See footnote 3.

the bank to undue risks or hinder effective supervision. The supervisor determines that the bank has, from the outset, adequate financial and organisational resources to handle the acquisition/ investment.

4. Laws or regulations clearly define for which cases a notification after the acquisition or investment is sufficient. Such cases should primarily refer to activities closely related to banking and the investment being small relative to the bank's capital.

Principle 6: **Banking supervisors must set minimum capital adequacy requirements for banks that reflect the risks that the latter undertake and must define the components of capital, bearing in mind its ability to absorb losses. For internationally active banks, these requirements must not be less than those established in the Basel Capital Accord.**

Essential criteria

1. Laws or regulations require all banks to calculate and maintain consistently a minimum capital adequacy ratio. At least for internationally active banks, the definition of capital, method of calculation and the ratio required are not lower than those established in the Basel Capital Accord.
2. The required capital ratio reflects the risk profile of individual banks, in particular the credit and market risk. Both on and off-balance-sheet risks are included.
3. The laws or regulations or the supervisor define the components of capital, ensuring that emphasis is given to those elements of capital available for absorbing losses.
4. Capital adequacy ratios are calculated and applied on a consolidated bank basis.

5. Laws or regulations clearly give the supervisor the authority to take measures should a bank fall below the minimum CAR.

6. Regular (at least by annual) reporting by banks to the supervisor is required on capital ratios and their components.

Additional criteria

1. For domestic, as well as internationally active banks, the definition of capital is broadly consistent with the Basel Capital Accord.

2. The supervisor clearly sets out the actions to be taken if capital falls below the minimum standards.

3. The supervisor determines that banks have an internal process for assessing their overall capital adequacy in relation to their risk profile.

4. Capital adequacy requirements take into account the conditions under which the banking system operates. Consequently, minimum requirements may be higher than the Basel Accord.

5. Capital adequacy ratios are calculated on both a consolidated and a solo basis for the banking entities within a banking group.

6. Laws or regulations stipulate the minimum absolute amount of capital for banks.

(Reference document: *"International convergence of capital measurement and capital standards"* July, 1988)

Principle 7: An essential part of any supervisory system is the independent evaluation of a bank's policies, practices and procedures related to the granting of loans and the making of investments as well as the ongoing management of the loan and investment portfolios.

Essential criteria

1. The supervisor requires and periodically verifies that prudent credit granting and investment criteria, policies, practices and procedures are approved, implemented and periodically reviewed by the bank management and boards of directors[5].

2. The supervisor requires and periodically verifies that such policies, practices and procedures include the establishment of an appropriate and properly controlled credit risk environment including:

   - a sound and well-documented credit granting and investment process;
   - the maintenance of an appropriate credit administration, measurement and ongoing monitoring/reporting process (including asset grading/classification); and
   - ensuring adequate controls over credit risk.

3. The supervisor requires and periodically verifies that banks make credit decisions free of conflicting interests on an arm's length basis and free from inappropriate pressure from outside parties. (This aspect of banking activity has been dealt with in part II (C & D).

[5] This paper refers to a management structure composed of a board of directors and senior management. The Committee is aware that there are significant differences in the legislative and regulatory framework across countries as regards the functions of the board of directors and the senior management. In some countries, the board has the main, if not exclusive, function of supervising the executive body (senior as well as general management) so as to ensure that the latter fulfils all its tasks. For this reason, in some cases, it is known as a supervisory board. This means that the board has no executive functions. In other countries, by contrast, the board has a broader competence in that it lays down the general framework for the management of the bank. Owing to these differences, the notions of the board of directors and the senior management are used in this paper not to identify legal provisions but rather to classify two decision-making functions within a bank.

4. The supervisor requires that essentially a bank's credit assessment and granting standards are communicated to all personnel involved in credit granting activities.

5. The supervisor has full access to information in the credit and investment portfolios and to the lending officers of the bank.

Additional criteria

1. The supervisor requires the credit policy to prescribe that major advances or investments, exceeding a certain amount or percentage of the bank's capital, are decided at a high managerial level of the bank. The same applies to advances or investments that are especially risky or otherwise not in line with the mainstream of the bank's activities.

2. The supervisor requires that banks have management information systems that provide essential details on the condition of the loan and investment portfolios.

3. The supervisor verifies that the bank management monitors the total indebtedness of entities to which credit is extended.

(Reference document: "*Principles for the Management of Credit Risk*", July 1999.)

Principle 8: Banking supervisors must be satisfied that banks establish and adhere to a set of adequate policies, practices and procedures for evaluating the quality of assets and the adequacy of loan loss provisions and reserves.

Essential criteria

1. Either the laws or regulations or the supervisor set the rules for periodic review by banks of their individual advances, asset classification and provisioning or the laws/regulations establish a

general framework and require banks to formulate specific policies for dealing with problem loans.

2. The classification and provisioning policies of a bank and their implementation are regularly reviewed by the supervisor or external auditors.

3. The system for classification and provisioning includes off-balance-sheet exposures.

4. The supervisor determines that banks have appropriate policies and procedures to ensure that loan loss provisions and write-offs reflect realistic repayment expectations.

5. The supervisor determines that banks have appropriate procedures and organisational resources for the ongoing overseeing of problem advances and for collecting past dues.

6. The supervisor has the authority to require a bank to strengthen its lending practices, credit granting standards, level of provisions and reserves and the overall financial strength if it deems the level of problem assets to be of concern.

7. The supervisor is informed on a periodic basis and in relevant detail concerning the classification of loans and assets and provisioning.

8. The supervisor requires banks to have mechanisms in place for continually assessing the strength of guarantees and appraising the worth of collateral.

9. Loans are required to be identified as impaired when there is reason to believe that all amounts due (both principal and interest) will not be collected in accordance with the contractual terms of the loan agreement.

10. The valuation of collateral is required to reflect the net realisable value.

Additional criteria

1. Loans are required to be classified when payments are contractually a minimum number of days in arrears (e.g., 30, 60 or 90 days). Refinancing of loans that would otherwise fall into arrears does not lead to improved classifications for such loans.

2. The supervisor requires that valuation, classification and provisioning for large advances are conducted on an individual item basis.

(Reference document: "*Sound Practices for Loan Accounting and Disclosure*", July 1999.)

Principle 9: Banking supervisors must be satisfied that banks have management information systems that enable the management to identify concentrations within the portfolio and supervisors must set prudential limits to restrict bank exposures to single borrowers or groups of related borrowers.

Essential criteria

1. A closely related group is explicitly defined to reflect the actual risk exposure[6]. The supervisor has discretion, which may be prescribed by law, in interpreting this definition on a case-by-case basis.

2. The laws, regulations or the supervisor set prudent limits on large exposures to a single borrower or a closely related group of borrowers. Exposures include all claims and transactions, on - as well as off-balance sheet.

---

[6] The definition can include not only legally related companies but also financially related companies, e.g., with common ownership. Also, physical persons are considered as being parts of closely related groups, e.g. when they have large economic interests at stake in the groups (for instance, when they are large shareholders).

3. The supervisor verifies that banks have management information systems that enable the management to identify on a timely basis concentrations (including large individual exposures) within the portfolio on an individual as well as a consolidated basis.
4. The supervisor verifies that the bank management monitors these limits and that these are not exceeded both on an individual and a consolidated basis.
5. The supervisor regularly obtains information that enables concentrations within a bank's credit portfolio, including sectoral and geographic exposures, to be reviewed.

Additional criteria

1. Banks are required to adhere to the following definitions:
   - Ten per cent or more of a bank's capital is defined as a large exposure;
   - Twenty five per cent of a bank's capital is the limit for an individual large exposure to a private sector non-bank borrower or a closely related group of borrowers.

Minor deviations from these limits may be acceptable, especially if these are explicitly temporary or related to very small or specialised banks only.

(Reference document: "*Measuring and controlling large credit exposures*", January 1991.)

Principle 10: In order to prevent abuses arising from connected lending, supervisors must have in place requirements that banks lend to related companies and individuals on an arm's-length basis and that such extensions of credit are effectively monitored and other appropriate steps are taken to control or mitigate the risks.

Essential criteria

1. A comprehensive definition of connected or related parties exists in law and/or regulation. The supervisor has discretion, which may be prescribed in law, to make judgements about the existence of connections between the bank and other parties.

2. Laws and regulations are there to ensure that exposures to connected or related parties may not be extended on more favourable terms (i.e., for credit assessment, tenor, interest rates, amortisation schedules and requirement for collateral) than corresponding loans to non-related counterparties[7].

3. The supervisor requires that transactions with connected or related parties exceeding specified amounts or otherwise posing special risks are subject to approval by the bank's board of directors.

4. The supervisor requires that banks have procedures in place to prevent persons benefiting from the loan being part of the preparation of the loan assessment or of the decision itself.

5. The laws or regulations set or the supervisor have the mandate to set on a general or case-by-case basis, limits for loans to connected and related parties, to deduct such lending from capital when assessing the capital adequacy or to require collateralisation of such loans.

6. The supervisor requires banks to have information systems to identify individual loans to connected and related parties as well as the total amount of such

---

[7] An exception may be appropriate for beneficial terms that are part of the overall remuneration packages (e.g., employees receive credit at favourable rates.)

loans and to monitor these through an independent credit administration process.

7. The supervisor obtains and reviews information on aggregate lending to connected and related parties.

Additional criteria

1. The definition of connected or related parties established in law and/or regulation is broad and generally includes affiliated companies, significant shareholders, board members, senior management, key staff as well as close family members, the corresponding persons in affiliated companies and companies controlled by insiders and shareholders.
2. There are limits on aggregate exposures to connected and related parties that are at least as strict as those for single borrowers, groups or related borrowers.

Principle 11: Banking supervisors must be satisfied that banks have adequate policies and procedures for identifying, monitoring and controlling country risk and transfer risk in their international lending and investment activities and for maintaining appropriate reserves against such risks.

Essential criteria

1. The supervisor determines that a bank's policies and procedures give due regard to the identification, monitoring and control of country and transfer risk. Exposures are identified and monitored on an individual country basis (in addition to the end-borrower/end-counterparty basis). Banks are required to monitor and evaluate developments in country and transfer risk and apply appropriate counter-measures.

2. The supervisor verifies that banks have information systems, risk management systems and internal control systems to comply with those policies.

3. There is a supervisory overseeing of the setting of appropriate provisions against country and transfer risk. There are different international practices which are all acceptable as long as these lead to reasonable, risk-related results. These include, *inter alia*:

   - The supervisor (or some other official authority) decides on appropriate minimum provisioning by setting fixed percentages for exposures to each country.

   - The supervisor (or some other official authority) sets percentage ranges for each country and the banks may decide, within these ranges, which provisioning to apply for the individual exposures.

   - The bank itself (or some other body such as the national bankers' association) sets percentages or guidelines or even decides for each individual loan on the appropriate provisioning. The provisioning will then be judged by the external auditor and/or by the supervisor.

4. The supervisor obtains and reviews sufficient information on a timely basis on the country risk/transfer risk of individual banks.

(Reference document: "*Management of banks' international lending*", March 1982.)

Principle 12: Banking supervisors must be satisfied that banks have in place systems that accurately measure, monitor and adequately control market risks; supervisors should have powers to impose specific limits and /or a specific capital charge on market risk exposures, if warranted.

Essential criteria

1. The supervisor determines that a bank has suitable policies and procedures related to the identification, measuring, monitoring and control of market risk.
2. The supervisor determines that the bank has set appropriate limits for various market risks, including their foreign exchange business.
3. The supervisor has the power to impose a specific capital charge and/or specific limits on market risk exposures, including their foreign exchange business.
4. The supervisor verifies that banks have information systems, risk management systems and internal control systems to comply with those policies, and also that the limits (either internal or imposed by the supervisor) are strictly adhered to.
5. The supervisor satisfies itself that there are systems and controls in place to ensure that all transactions are captured on a timely basis and that the banks' positions are revalued frequently, using reliable and prudent market data.
6. The supervisor determines that banks perform scenario analysis, stress testing and contingency planning, as deemed appropriate, as well as periodic validation or testing of the systems used to measure market risk.
7. The supervisor has the expertise needed to monitor the actual level of complexity in the market activities of banks.

Additional criteria

1. Either through on-site work, internal or independent external experts, the supervisor determines that the senior management understands the market risks

inherent in the business lines/products traded and that it regularly reviews and understands the implications (and limitations) of the risk management information that they receive.

2. The supervisor reviews the quality of management information and forms an opinion on whether the management information is sufficient to reflect properly the banks' position and exposure to market risk. In particular, the supervisor reviews the assumptions the management has used in the stress testing scenarios and the banks' contingency plans for dealing with such conditions.

3. The supervisor, who does not have access to adequate skills and capacity, does not allow banks to determine their regulatory capital requirements based on sophisticated models.

(Reference document: "*Amendment to the Capital Accord to incorporate market risks*", January 1996.)

Principle 13: Supervisors must be satisfied that banks have in place a comprehensive risk management process (including an appropriate board and senior management perusal) to identify, measure, monitor and control all other material risks and, where appropriate, to hold capital against these risks.

Essential criteria

1. The supervisor requires individual banks to have in place comprehensive risk management processes to identify, measure, monitor and control material risks. These processes are adequate for the size and nature of the activities of the bank and are periodically adjusted in the light of the changing risk profile of the bank and external market developments. These processes include appropriate board and senior management scrutiny.

2. The supervisor determines that the risk management processes address liquidity risk, interest rate risk and operational as well as all other risks including those covered in other principles (e.g., credit and market risk). These would include:

    - Liquidity: good management information systems, central liquidity control, analysis of net funding requirements under alternative scenarios, diversification of funding sources, stress testing and contingency planning. Liquidity management should separately address domestic and foreign currencies.
    - Interest rate risk: good management information systems and stress testing.
    - Operational risk: internal audit, procedures to counter fraud, sound business resumption plans, procedures covering major system modifications and preparation for significant changes in the business environment.

3. The supervisor issues standards related to such topics as liquidity, interest rate, foreign exchange and operational risks.
4. The supervisor sets liquidity guidelines for banks, which include allowing only truly liquid assets to be treated as such and take into consideration undrawn commitments and other off-balance- sheet liabilities as well as existing on-balance-sheet liabilities.
5. The supervisor determines that limits and procedures are communicated to the appropriate personnel and the primary responsibility for adhering to limits and procedures is placed with the relevant business units.
6. The supervisor periodically verifies that these risk management processes, capital requirements,

liquidity guidelines and qualitative standards are being strictly adhered to in practice.

Additional criteria

1. The supervisor has the authority to require a bank to hold capital against risks in addition to credit and market risk.
2. The supervisor encourages banks to include a statement on their risk management policies and procedures in their publicly available accounts.
3. Supervisors obtain sufficient information to enable them to identify those institutions carrying out significant foreign currency liquidity transformation.
4. The supervisor determines that where a bank conducts its business in multiple currencies, the management understands and addresses the particular issues this involves. The foreign currency liquidity strategy is separately stress-tested and the results of such tests are a factor in determining the appropriateness of mismatches.

(Reference documents: *"Principles for the management of interest rate risk"*, September 1997 and *"A framework for measuring and managing liquidity"*, September 1992.)

Principle 14: Banking supervisors must determine that banks have in place internal controls that are adequate for the nature and scale of their business. These should include clear arrangements for: delegating authority and responsibility; separation of the functions that involve committing the banks to paying away their funds and accounting for their assets and liabilities; reconciliation of these processes; safeguarding their assets; and appropriate independent internal or external audit and compliance functions to test adherence to these controls as well as applicable laws and regulations.

Essential criteria

1. Corporate or banking laws identify the responsibilities of the board of directors with respect to corporate governance principles to ensure that there is effective control over every aspect of risk management.

2. The supervisor determines that banks have in place internal controls that are adequate for the nature and scale of their business. These controls are the responsibility of the board of directors and deal with the organisational structure, accounting procedures, checks and balances and the safeguarding of assets and investments. More specifically, these address:

   - Organisational structure: definitions of duties and responsibilities — these include a clear delegation of authority (for example, clear loan approval limits), decision-making procedures and separation of critical functions (for example, business origination, payments, reconciliation, risk management, accounting, audit and compliance).

   - Accounting procedures: reconciliation of accounts, control lists and information for management.

   - Checks and balances (or "four eyes principles"): segregation of duties, cross- checking, dual control of assets and double signatures.

   - Safeguarding assets and investments: including physical control.

3. To achieve a strong control environment, the supervisor requires that the board of directors and the senior management of a bank understand the underlying risks in their business and are both committed to and are legally responsible for the

control environment. Consequently, the supervisor evaluates the composition of the board of directors and the senior management to determine that they have the necessary skills for the size and nature of the activities of the bank and can address the changing risk profile of the bank and external market developments. The supervisor has the legal authority to require changes in the composition of the board and management in order to satisfy these criteria.

4. The supervisor determines that there is an appropriate balance in the skills and resources of the back office and control functions relative to the front office/ business origination.

5. The supervisor determines that banks have an appropriate audit function charged with (a) ensuring that policies and procedures are complied with and (b) reviewing whether the existing policies, practices and controls remain sufficient and appropriate for the bank's business. The supervisor determines that the audit function:

   - has unfettered access to the bank's business lines and support departments;
   - has appropriate independence, including reporting lines to the board of directors and status within the bank to ensure that the senior management reacts to and acts upon its recommendations;
   - has sufficient resources and staff that are suitably trained and have relevant experience to understand and evaluate the business they are auditing;
   - employs a methodology that identifies the key risks run by the bank and allocates its resources accordingly.

6. The supervisor has access to the reports of the audit function.

Additional criteria

1. In those countries with an unicameral board structure (as opposed to a bicameral structure with a supervisory as well as a management board), the supervisor requires the board of directors to include a number of experienced non-executive directors.
2. The supervisor requires the internal audit function to report to an Audit Committee.
3. In those countries with an unicameral board structure, the supervisor requires the Audit Committee to include experienced non-executive directors.

(Reference document: "*Framework for internal control systems in banking organisations*", September 1998.)

Principle 15: Banking supervisors must determine that banks have adequate policies, practices and procedures in place, including strict "know-your-customer" rules, that promote high ethical and professional standards in the financial sector and prevent the banks being from used, intentionally or unintentionally, by criminal elements.

Essential criteria

1. The supervisor determines that banks have in place adequate policies, practices and procedures that promote high ethical and professional standards and prevent the banks from being used, intentionally or unintentionally, by criminal elements. This includes the prevention and detection of criminal activity or fraud and reporting of such suspected activities to the appropriate authorities.
2. The supervisor determines that banks have documented and enforced policies for identification

of customers and those acting on their behalf as part of their anti-money-laundering programme. There are clear rules on what records must be kept on customer identification and individual transactions as also the retention period.

3. The supervisor determines that banks have formal procedures to recognise potentially suspicious transactions. These might include additional authorisation for large cash (or similar) deposits or withdrawals and special procedures for unusual transactions.

4. The supervisor determines that banks appoint a senior officer with explicit responsibility for ensuring that the bank's policies and procedures are, at the very minimum, in accordance with local statutory and regulatory anti-money laundering requirements.

5. The supervisor determines that banks have clear procedures, communicated to all personnel, for staff to report suspicious transactions to the dedicated senior officer responsible for anti-money laundering compliance.

6. The supervisor determines that banks have established lines of communication both to the management and to an internal security department or a guardian for reporting problems.

7. In addition to filing complaints with the appropriate criminal authorities, banks report to the supervisor suspicious activities and incidents of fraud bearing on the safety, soundness or reputation of the bank.

8. Laws, regulations and/or banks' policies ensure that a member of staff who reports suspicious transactions in good faith to a dedicated senior officer and the internal security department or directly to the relevant authority cannot be held liable.

9. The supervisor periodically checks that banks' money laundering controls and systems for preventing, identifying and reporting frauds are sufficient. The supervisor has adequate enforcement powers (regulatory and/or criminal prosecution) to take action against a bank that does not comply with its anti-money laundering obligations.

10. The supervisor is able, directly or indirectly, to share with domestic and foreign financial sector supervisory authorities information related to suspected or actual criminal activities.

11. The supervisor determines that banks have a policy statement on ethics and professional behaviour that is clearly communicated to all members of staff.

Additional criteria

1. The laws and/or regulations embody sound practices that are in vogue internationally, such as compliance with the relevant Financial Action Task Force Recommendations issued in 1990 (revised in 1996).

2. The supervisor determines that bank staff is adequately trained on money laundering detection and prevention.

3. The supervisor has the legal obligation to inform the relevant criminal authorities of any suspicious transactions.

4. The supervisor is able, directly or indirectly, to share with the concerned judicial authorities information related to suspected or actual criminal activities.

5. The supervisor has access to in-house resources particularly expertise on financial fraud and anti-money laundering obligations.

(Reference document: "*Prevention of criminal use of the*

banking system for the purpose of money-laundering", December 1988.)

Principle 16: An effective system should consist of some measures of both on-site and off-site supervision.

(Note: this principle should be considered in conjunction with principles 17 to 20.)

Essential criteria

1. Banking supervision requires in-depth understanding, periodical analysis and evaluation of individual banks, focussing on safety and soundness, based on meetings with the management and a combination of both on-site and off-site supervision. The supervisor has a framework that (1) uses on-site work (conducted either by its own staff or through the work of external auditors) as a primary tool to:

   - provide independent verification that adequate corporate governance (including risk management and internal control systems) exists in individual banks;
   - determine that the information provided by banks is reliable;
   - obtain additional information needed to assess the condition of the bank.

2. And (2) uses off-site work as a primary tool to:

   - review and analyse the financial condition of individual banks using prudential reports, statistical returns and other appropriate information, including publicly available information;
   - monitor trends and developments for the banking sector as a whole.

3. The supervisor checks compliance with prudential regulations and other legal requirements through on-site and off-site work.
4. The appropriate mix of on-site and off-site supervision is determined by the particular conditions and circumstances of the country. In any event, the framework integrates the two functions so as to maximise the synergy and avoid supervisory gaps.

Additional criteria

1. The supervisor has procedures in place to assess the effectiveness of on-site and off-site functions and to address any weaknesses that are identified.
2. The supervisor has the right to access copies of reports submitted to the board by both internal and external auditors.
3. The supervisor has a methodology for determining and assessing the nature, importance and scope of the risks to which individual banks are exposed, including the business focus, risk profile and the internal control environment. Off-site and on-site work is prioritised based on the results of that assessment.
4. The supervisor is legally required to treat as confidential any information received as part of the supervisory process. However, this functionary is given powers under the law to disclose information in certain defined circumstances. The law prevents disclosure of confidential information unless the supervisor is satisfied that it will be held confidential by the recipient or unless disclosure is otherwise required by law.
5. The supervisor is able to reasonably place reliance on

internal audit work that has been competently and independently performed.

Principle 17: Banking supervisors must have regular contact with bank management and a thorough understanding of the institution's operations.

Essential criteria

1. Based on the risk profile of individual banks, the supervisor has a programme of regular meetings with members of both senior and middle management (including the board, non-executive directors and heads of individual units) to discuss operational matters such as strategy, group structure, corporate governance, performance, capital adequacy, liquidity, asset quality, risk management systems etc.
2. The supervisor has a thorough understanding of the activities of its banks. This is accomplished through a combination of off-site surveillance, on-site reviews and regular meetings.
3. The supervisor requires banks to notify any substantive changes in their activities or any material adverse developments, including breach of legal and prudential requirements.
4. As part of the licensing process and on an on-going basis during routine supervision, the supervisor evaluates the quality of management.

Principle 18: Banking supervisors must have a mechanism for collecting, reviewing and analysing prudential reports and statistical returns from banks on an individual as well as consolidated basis[8].

---

[8] This core principle refers to *accounting consolidation*, which should be applied by one means or another to the whole bank, i.e. not only to the figures of a bank's branches but also to those subsidiaries in which the bank has a significant controlling interest.

Essential criteria

1. The supervisor has the legal authority to require banking organisations to submit information, on both an individual and a consolidated basis, on their financial condition and performance, at regular intervals. These reports provide data on matters such as on-and off-balance sheet assets and liabilities, profit and loss, capital adequacy, liquidity, large exposures, loan loss provisioning, market risk and deposit sources.

2. Either laws and regulations or the supervisor have the authority to establish the principles and norms regarding the consolidation of accounts as well as the accounting techniques to be used.

3. The supervisor has a mechanism for enforcing compliance with the requirement that the information be submitted on a timely and accurate basis. The supervisor determines that the appropriate level of senior management is responsible for the accuracy of supervisory returns, can impose penalties for deliberate mis-reporting and persistent errors and can require that inaccurate information be amended.

4. The information that is required to be submitted includes standardised prudential and statistical reports and detailed balance sheets and income statements as well as supporting schedules that provide details concerning on-and off-balance sheet activities and reserves included in the capital. Inclusion of data on loan classification and provisioning is also required.

5. The supervisor has the authority to request and receive any relevant information from banks as well as any of their related companies, irrespective of their activities, where the supervisor believes that it is

material to the financial situation of the banks or the assessment of their risks.

6. The supervisor has an analytical framework that uses the statistical and prudential information for the ongoing monitoring of the condition and performance of individual banks. The results are also used as a component of on-site supervision planning. This requires that the supervisor has an adequate information system.

7. In order to make meaningful comparisons between banking organisations, the supervisor collects data from all banks and all other relevant entities within a banking organisation on a comparable basis and related to the same dates (stock data) and periods (flow data).

8. The supervisor collects data from banks (on a monthly, quarterly and annual basis) commensurate with the nature of the information requested and the size, activities and risk profile of the individual bank.

Principle 19: Banking supervisors must have a means of independent validation of supervisory information either through on-site examinations or use of external auditors.

Essential criteria

1. The supervisor has in place a coherent process for planning and executing on-site visits, using either in-house examiners or external auditors, whichever is appropriate. There are policies and procedures in place to ensure that examinations are conducted on a thorough and consistent basis with clear responsibilities, objectives and outputs. The supervisor holds meetings with banks and their auditors to discuss reports of the work by the external auditors and to agree on the responsibilities for corrective action.

2. The supervisor has the authority to monitor the quality of work done by external auditors for supervisory purposes. The supervisor has the authority to appoint directly external auditors for conducting supervisory tasks or oppose the appointment of an external auditor deemed to have inappropriate expertise and/or lacking in independence.

3. The supervisor can also make use of external auditors to examine specific aspects of the banks' operations, provided there is a well developed, professionally independent auditing and accounting profession with skills to undertake the work required. The respective roles and responsibilities for the supervisor and auditors in these circumstances are clearly defined by the supervisor.

4. The supervisor has the legal right of full access to all bank records for the furtherance of supervisory work. The supervisor also has similar access to the board, the senior management and staff, where required.

5. The supervisor has a programme for the periodic examination of supervisory returns by examiners or through the work of external auditors. There is a requirement that certain key supervisory returns such as that for capital adequacy be examined at least annually by the auditors and a report submitted to the supervisor.

Additional criteria

1. The supervisor meets the members of management and the board of directors each year to discuss the results of the supervisory examination or the external audit. Such visits should allow for the supervisor to meet separately the independent board members.

2. The supervisor meets periodically external audit firms

to discuss issues of common interest relating to bank operations.

(Reference document: *"The relationship between bank supervisors and external auditors"*, July 1989.)

Principle 20: An essential element of banking supervision is the ability of supervisors to oversee the banking group on a consolidated basis[9].

Essential criteria

1. The supervisor is aware of the overall structure of banking organisations (i.e., the bank and its subsidiaries) or groups and has an understanding of the activities of all material parts of these groups, including those that are supervised directly by other agencies.

2. The supervisor has the appropriate framework that evaluates the risks that the non-banking activities conducted by a bank or banking group may pose.

3. The supervisor has the legal authority to review the overall activities of a bank, whether the activities are conducted directly (including those conducted in overseas offices) or indirectly through subsidiaries and affiliates of the bank.

4. There are no impediments to the direct or indirect supervision of all affiliates and subsidiaries of a banking organisation.

5. Laws or regulations establish, or the supervisor has the authority to impose, prudential standards on a

[9] Supervision of the banking group on a consolidated basis goes beyond accounting consolidation. It implies that there is a group-wide approach to supervision whereby all the risks run by a banking group are taken into account, wherever these are booked. It is important to note that both accounting consolidation and consolidated supervision are key aspects of the supervision of banking groups.

consolidated basis for the banking organisation. The supervisor uses the authority to establish prudential standards on a consolidated basis to cover such areas as capital adequacy, large exposures and lending limits.

6. The supervisor collects consolidated financial information for each banking organisation.

7. The supervisor has arrangements with the functional regulators of individual business vehicles within a banking organisation or group to receive information on the financial condition and adequacy of risk management as well as controls on such business vehicles.

8. The supervisor has the authority to limit or circumscribe the range of activities the consolidated banking group may conduct and the overseas locations in which these can be conducted; the supervisor uses this authority to determine that the activities are properly supervised and that the safety and soundness of the banking organisation are not ever compromised.

Additional criteria

1. For those countries that allow corporate ownership of banking companies:

   - the supervisor has the authority to review the activities of parent companies and those affiliated with the former and utilises the authority in practice to determine the safety and soundness of the bank;

   - the supervisor has the authority to take all remedial actions including ring-fencing, regarding parent companies and non-bank affiliates, concerning matters that could affect the safety and soundness of the bank; and

- the supervisor has the authority to establish and enforce fit and proper standards for the owners and the senior management of parent companies.

(Reference documents: "*Consolidated supervision of banks' international activities*", March 1979; "*The supervision of cross-border banking*", October 1996.)

Principle 21: Banking supervisors must be satisfied that each bank maintains adequate records drawn up in accordance with consistent accounting policies and practices that enable the supervisor to obtain a true and fair view of the financial condition of the bank and the profitability of its business, and that the bank publishes on a regular basis financial statements that fairly reflect its condition.

Essential criteria

1. The supervisor has the authority to hold the management responsible for ensuring that financial record keeping systems and the data they produce are reliable, and that the required reports are submitted on a timely and accurate basis.
2. The supervisor has the authority to hold the management responsible for ensuring that the management report and financial statements issued annually to the public receive proper external verification and bear an external auditor's opinion.
3. The supervisor ensures that information from bank records is verified periodically through on-site examinations and/or external audits.
4. The supervisor ensures that there are open communication lines with the external auditors.
5. The supervisor provides report instructions that clearly establish the accounting standards to be used in preparing supervisory reports. Such standards are

based on accounting principles and rules that command wide international acceptance and are aimed specifically at banking institutions.

6. The supervisor requires banks to utilise valuation rules that are consistent, realistic and prudent, taking account of current values where relevant, and that profits are net of appropriate provisions.

7. The laws or regulations set, or alternatively, the supervisor has the authority, in appropriate circumstances, to establish the scope and standards to be achieved in the external audits of individual banks and to make public issue of individual bank financial statements subject to prior approval.

8. The supervisor enjoys the discretion to treat as confidential certain types of sensitive information.

9. The supervisor requires banks to produce annual audited financial statements based on accounting principles and rules that command wide international acceptance and have been audited in accordance with internationally accepted auditing practices and standards.

10. The supervisor has the right to revoke the appointment of a bank's auditors, where justified.

11. Where supervisors rely primarily on the work of external auditors (rather than on their own examination staff), banks are required to appoint auditors who are recognised by the supervisor as having the necessary professional skills and independence to perform the work.

Additional criteria

1. The supervisor promotes periodical public disclosures of information that are timely, accurate and sufficiently

comprehensive to provide a basis for effective market discipline.

2. The supervisor has guidelines covering the scope and conduct of audit programmes, which ensure that audits cover such areas as the loan portfolio, loan loss reserves, non-performing assets, asset valuation, trading and other securities activities, derivatives, asset securitisation and the adequacy of internal controls over financial reporting.

3. Auditors have a legal duty to report to the supervisor matters of material significance — for example, a failure to maintain the licensing criteria or breaches of banking or other laws. The law protects auditors from any breach of confidentiality when such information is communicated in good faith.

4. Auditors also are legally bound to report to the supervisor matters which, in the context of the available information, they deem likely to be of material significance to the functions of the supervisor.

Principle 22: Banking supervisors must have at their disposal adequate supervisory measures to bring about timely corrective action when banks fail to meet prudential requirements (such as minimum capital adequacy ratios) or there are regulatory violations and depositors are otherwise threatened. In extreme circumstances, this should even include revoking the banking licence or recommending its revocation.

Essential criteria

1. The supervisor has the authority, backed by legal sanctions, to take an appropriate range of remedial actions against — and impose penalties upon — banks depending on the severity of a situation. Such actions are used to address problems like a failure to meet prudential requirements or violations of

regulations. These cover informal, oral and written communications to bank managements as well as actions that involve the revocation of the banking licence.

2. The range of possible actions available also extends to restricting the current activities of the bank, withholding approval of new activities or acquisitions, restricting or suspending payments to shareholders or share repurchases, curbing asset transfers, barring individuals from taking up banking, replacing or restricting the powers of managers, directors, or controlling interests, arranging a take-over by or merger with a healthier institution and imposing conservatorship.

3. The supervisor ensures that remedial actions are taken in a timely manner.

4. The supervisor applies penalties and sanctions not only to the bank, but, when and if necessary, also to management and/or the board of directors.

Additional criteria

1. Laws and/or regulations mitigate against the supervisor, unduly delaying appropriate corrective actions.

2. The supervisor addresses all significant remedial actions in a written document submitted to the board of directors and requires that progress reports are given in writing as well.

Principle 23: Banking supervisors must practise globally consolidated supervision over their internationally active banking organisations, adequately monitoring and applying appropriate prudential norms to all aspects of the business conducted by these organisations worldwide, primarily at their foreign branches, joint ventures and subsidiaries.

Essential criteria

1. The supervisor has the authority to supervise the overseas activities of locally incorporated banks.

2. The supervisor satisfies itself that management is maintaining a close watch over the bank's foreign branches, joint ventures and subsidiaries and also that the local management of any overseas office has the necessary expertise to manage those operations in a safe and sound manner.

3. The supervisor ensures that the bank management's scrutiny includes: a) information reporting on its overseas operations which is adequate in scope and frequency and is periodically verified; b) assessing in an appropriate manner compliance with internal controls and c) ensuring effective local control of foreign operations.

4. The home country supervisor has the authority to require closure of overseas offices or imposing limits on their activities if it is deemed that the control of a local operation by the bank and/or by the host country supervisor is not adequate relative to the risks involved.

Additional criteria

1. The supervisor has a policy for assessing whether it needs to conduct on-site examinations or requires additional reporting and it has the legal authority and resources to take those steps as and when appropriate.

2. The supervisor sees to it that the management's local control of foreign operations is particularly close when these activities have a higher risk profile and/ or when these differ fundamentally from those conducted on home territory or are conducted at

locations that are especially remote from the principal locations at which the bank conducts comparable activities.

3. The supervisor arranges to visit the offshore locations periodically, the frequency being determined by the size and risk profile of the overseas operation. The supervisor meets the local supervisors during these visits.

4. The home country supervisor assesses the quality of supervision in countries in which its banks have material operations.

(Reference documents: "*Principles for the supervision of banks' foreign establishments*", May 1983; "*Minimum standards for the supervision of international banking groups and their cross-border establishments*", July 1992; "*The supervision of cross-border banking*", October 1996.)

Principle 24: A key component of consolidated supervision is establishing contact and information exchange with the other supervisors involved, primarily those in the host country.

Essential criteria

1. Where the overseas operations of a bank are of a significant magnitude, the home country supervisor establishes informal or formal arrangements (such as memoranda of understanding) with host country supervisors for appropriate information-sharing on the financial condition and performance of these operations in the host country. Information sharing arrangements with host country supervisors include being advised of adverse assessments of such aspects of a bank's operations as the quality of risk management and controls at the offices in the host country.

2. The supervisor can prohibit banks or their affiliates from establishing operations in countries with secrecy laws or other regulations prohibiting flows of information deemed necessary for effective supervision.

3. The home supervisor provides information to host country supervisors on specific offices in the host country concerning the overall framework of supervision in which the banking group operates, and, to the extent appropriate, on significant problems arising in the head office or in the group as a whole.

Additional criteria

1. A supervisor taking consequential action on the basis of information received from another such functionary consults the latter to the extent possible, beforehand.

2. Even for the less important overseas operations of a bank, the home country supervisor exchanges appropriate information with a similar authority in the host country.

(Reference documents: same as for principle 23.)

Principle 25: Banking supervisors must require the local operations of foreign banks to be conducted on the same high standards as are required of domestic institutions and must have the powers to share the information needed by the home country supervisors of those banks for the purpose of carrying out consolidated supervision.

Essential criteria

1. Local branches and subsidiaries of foreign banks are subject to similar prudential, inspection and regulatory reporting requirements as domestic banks.

2. For purposes of the licensing process as well as ongoing supervision, the host country supervisor

assesses whether the home country supervisor practises consolidated global supervision.

3. The host supervisor, before issuing a licence, ensures that an approval (or at least a no objection certificate) from the home supervisor has been received.

4. The host country supervisor can share with home country counterparts information about the local operations of foreign banks provided its confidentiality is protected.

5. Home country supervisors are given on-site access to local offices and subsidiaries for purposes of safety and soundness.

6. The host country supervisor advises home country supervisors on a timely basis of any substantive remedial action it takes regarding the operations of a bank in that country.

Additional criteria

1. The host country supervisor obtains from home country supervisors sufficient information on the banking group to allow it to put in proper perspective the activities conducted within its borders.

(Reference documents: same as for principle 23.)

AUTHOR'S COMMENTS

The core area of the criteria is the total autonomy of the supervisor. Rightly, the Basel Committee recognises that authority is not exercised by an individual but by a system. I presume that this stress on systemic supervision is entirely consistent with the spirit of effective control. But then, knowing that the world over — and not just in India — systems have failed time and again, expecting an ideal set-up to work as a matter of course does not seem the best way of attaining a high quality of banking performance generally.

The formation of the Basel Committee itself had been somewhat of a panic response to several improprieties committed by a number of transnational banking entities culminating in the wholesale repudiation of debt service commitments in 1982 by several Latin American and African countries. The international debt crisis of the time, which began with the Mexican Finance Minister formally declaring his nation's inability to service the massive debt it had run up, no doubt, demanded the most stringent supervision of banking activity. But then, the kind of gospel that the Basel Committee came up with must be proving too much to bank managements everywhere.

Nobody can be dismissive of prudence. Yes, banks must be prudent, but when healthy enterprise is the real need, bankers must strive for pragmatism. This would be better served by a mechanism that would promote growth of a high level of professionalism among bank managers at different levels. To say that this can be best achieved by threats, veiled or otherwise, does not consitute a sensible approach. Those who run the banks, on their own, must combine enterprise with responsibility. It is clear that the Basel Committee is lacking even the elementary trust of those, whose job it is to make the system work to the advantage of the community at large as much as the banks themselves. In making this observation, one is not disputing the wisdom of supervision *per se*, but only stressing the fact that the supervisory authority should motivate the bank officials into professional performance consistently. The Committee hardly has this in focus. Its attitude is one of the old time policeman who believes that only the stick would work. Yet, no system should be seen to work because of the fear the supervisor spread. What should, indeed, drive banking activity, both here and elsewhere, is the commitment of the person in the hot seat.

BRINGING DOWN THE CURTAINS

On a subject such as this, it is hardly easy to bring down the curtains at any point of time particularly in the present context of a largely unfinished reform agenda. Banks, no doubt, have done some spadework in terms of procedural changes and policy pronouncements. But, in the eleventh year of macro-economic reform, banks are still generally what they were in early 1991, not merely in terms of staff attitudes but also of policy and administrative reforms. The ethos are generally those of the long regulatory years.

While it is important that the preface should not read like a conclusion and *vice versa*, banking is one facet of the Indian economy that generally refuses to move with the changing times elsewhere. This should explain the striking similarity between the first and last pages. Yes, the internet is on display in some of the best run entities and money gets transferred from branch to branch in a matter of minutes. But, most constituents are apparently still in the middle ages, moved by a hand cart as it were. Dynamism is yet to become a feature of the Indian banking market place. If this seems a somewhat harsh winding up, this was but inevitable, given the state of things as of now. The Government is only partly to blame for this embarrassing scenario and much of the responsibility must vest with the multitude of men and women who supposedly sustain the banking system, though the bitter truth is that they only milk the system for their own benefit.

INDEX

❑❑❑